CHINA RISES

CHINA RISES

How China's Astonishing
Growth Will Change the World

John Farndon

This edition published by Virgin Books 2008

2 4 6 8 10 9 7 5 3

Copyright © John Farndon 2007, 2008

Maps copyright © Richard Horne 2007, 2008

John Farndon has asserted his right under the Copyright, Designs
and Patents Act 1988 to be identified as the author of this work

First published in Great Britain in 2007 by
Virgin Books
Random House
Thames Wharf Studios,
Rainville Road
London W6 9HA

www.rbooks.co.uk

Addresses for companies within The Random House Group Limited can be found at:
www.randomhouse.co.uk/offices.htm

The Random House Group Limited Reg. No. 954009

A CIP catalogue record for this book
is available from the British Library

ISBN 9780753513491

The Random House Group Limited supports The Forest Stewardship Council [FSC], the
leading international forest certification organisation. All our titles that are printed on
Greenpeace approved FSC certified paper carry the FSC logo.
Our paper procurement policy can be found at www.rbooks.co.uk/environment

Mixed Sources
Product group from well-managed
forests and other controlled sources
www.fsc.org Cert no. TT-COC-2139
© 1996 Forest Stewardship Council

FSC

Typeset by Phoenix Photosetting, Chatham, Kent
Printed in the UK by CPI Bookmarque, Croydon, CR0 4TD

CONTENTS

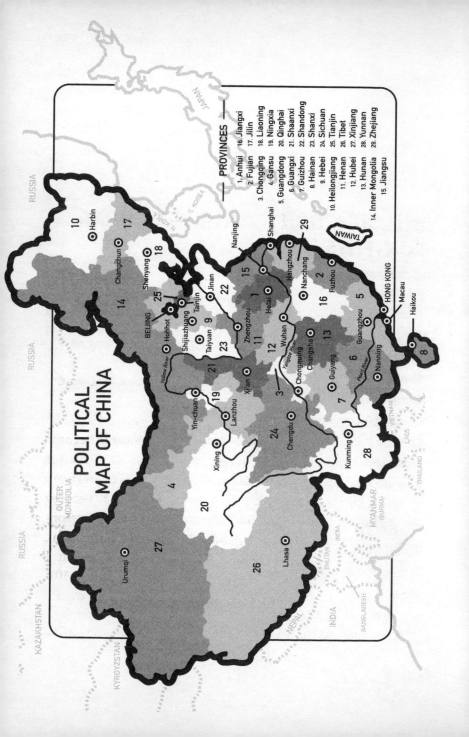

INTRODUCTION THE NEW CHINA

'It doesn't matter if it's a black cat or a white cat; as long as it can catch mice it's a good cat.'

Deng Xiaoping

On 18 June 2007, the unfinished Shanghai World Financial Centre overtopped the neighbouring Jinmao Tower to become the tallest building on the Chinese mainland at 423.8 metres (1,390 feet), compared with Jinmao's 420.5 metres (1,380 feet). By the time it was complete in March 2008, this 101-storey tower was the third tallest building in the world at an astonishing 492 metres (1,614 feet), eclipsed only by the Burj Dubai, which is due for completion in late 2008 and will reach a height of 531.3 metres (1,743 feet), and Taiwan's Taipei 101, which makes it to 508 metres (1,666 feet), but only with the aid of a 60-metre (197-feet) spire.

The Shanghai World Financial Centre is just one of the

skyscrapers going up in Shanghai's financial district of Pudong as it rolls out the biggest urban building programme the world has ever seen. With its huge population, China has always been able to build on a massive scale, as the Great Wall and the Grand Canal bear witness, but for a long time that ability has lain dormant. Now it is being unleashed again in Shanghai. Barely fifteen years ago, Pudong was open marsh and countryside. Today it is a city of 1.4 million people and swelling by the hour. Already, Pudong is eight times the size of Canary Wharf, London's financial district. Indeed, it's almost as big as the city of Chicago. And its skyline of state-of-the-art skyscrapers, designed by the world's top architects, have already begun to make New York's Manhattan look small and dated to many visitors winging in to Shanghai's new airport, and being whisked by the magnetic levitation train, the world's fastest train, into the city.

Building up China

It's not just Shanghai that is seeing this whirlwind of construction. Dozens of Chinese cities from Beijing to Shenzhen are being transformed as bulldozers and wrecking cranes trundle in to sweep away the old *hutongs* (lane houses) and shanty towns to clear the path for the multi-lane expressways, glitzy shopping malls and shimmering skyscrapers that are becoming a symbol of the new China. No developing nation has ever matched the amount of foreign investment that has come China's way in the last twenty years and no nation has ever had such a gigantic labour force to use to such dramatic effect.

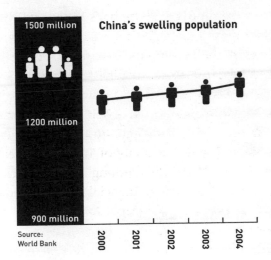

China's swelling population

1500 million

1200 million

900 million

Source:
World Bank

2000 2001 2002 2003 2004

China is currently home to a quarter of the world's population, and at the time when Europe was in the Dark Ages China was the world's most advanced civilisation by far. Yet for five hundred years its development has been lagging behind much of the rest of the world. All that is now changing. China is transforming itself at an astonishing rate. No longer a backwater, many fevered commentators proclaim, China could be set to dominate the world in the twenty-first century, overtaking the USA as the next superpower.

The statistics certainly are staggering. China's 1.3 billion citizens already have over three hundred million mobile phones and two hundred million Internet users. It's the world's largest producer of coal, steel and cement, the second largest consumer of energy and the third largest importer of

3

oil. It makes two-thirds of the world's photocopiers, microwave ovens, DVD players and shoes – and pretty much all the world's toys. More than half the world's cranes are busy at work in China helping to create the largest megacities the world has ever seen, with just one of these cities already home to more people than all of England. Indeed, Chinese people are moving from the rural interior into the booming coastal cities in what is by far the biggest human migration in the history of the world.

Consumer colossus or totalitarian titan?

In one way, China seems to be hurtling down the path to the consumer society at a pace and on a scale that has never been seen before. And some see it as an almost frightening triumph of western values. Yet, on the other hand, China remains in the hands of the same Communist Party that has ruled with an iron grip since 1949. More people in China live without an elected government than in the rest of the world put together. While most of the world has moved falteringly towards democracy, of a kind, China remains one of the few countries without an elected national government and without any guarantees of basic freedoms, and the memories of the Tiananmen Square massacre in 1989 are still raw.

There is no doubt that the whole issue of China and its place in the world has observers in the West excited. Documentaries, feature articles and magazine specials on the new China appear with ever increasing frequency in the media, and countless new books are hitting the bookstalls with titles such as *China Shakes the World*, *China: Friend or Foe?*, *The Changing Face of China* and *The Writing on the Wall*.

Oriental dream

On the one side are those who are excited by what is happening. Business pundits in particular seem to drool at the massive opportunities offered by the Chinese market. The startling growth of mobile-phone ownership, for instance, is cited as a sign of the riches to be earned once China's middle class has money to spend. With China's economy growing at almost 10 per cent a year and the country's city construction boom speeding up, the investment opportunities seem huge and copper-bottomed. Political pundits, meanwhile, note how far China's totalitarian Communist government has opened the country to market economics and individual aspirations. As Chinese people gain more and more economic freedom, they believe, so the pressure for political freedom and democracy will become irresistible. Some pundits even predict that China may become at least partially democratic within the next decade.

Yellow peril

On the other hand, there are those who see China's rise as frightening. On the business side, some are concerned that the western world will soon be swamped by China's economic power. Already the scale and cheapness of China's labour means that there are very few low-cost manufacturing industries where western businesses are able to compete with the Chinese. With simple goods like textiles, China already dominates the global market. Soon, even sophisticated manufactures like computers will go to China. Once China moves into services, as it threatens to do, the western economy is in real danger.

Another negative perspective is the view that the Chinese economic boom is simply unsustainable. It is a bubble based on massive loans, investment and expectations – but sooner or later the promises will have to be delivered. Then the bubble will burst, because China is really a country with eight hundred million poor people, not a giant lucrative market at all. When China's economic bubble bursts, as it must do sooner or later, it will plunge the world into a global recession worse than that of the 1930s.

On the political and strategic side, there are the worriers, especially among American neocons and Pentagon world-watchers, who argue that China could become an even bigger threat to world peace than Cold War Russia. They point out that China has long been a nuclear power, it has the world's largest standing army and that its military spending is rising by at least 10 per cent a year. Despite the reforms, they argue, China has remained a totalitarian Communist power. All prosperity is doing is giving China the means to throw its weight around.

Equally negative are those who point the finger at China's human-rights record, its level of repression, the widening gap between rich and poor, and the potentially appalling environmental costs of the country's breakneck development. They point out how China executes more people than any other country in the world, and how many millions of poor people's homes have been swept away in the building boom, and how many millions more have been left in beggary or unemployment by China's abandonment of welfare and its wind-down of state industries.

The China enigma

China has always attracted hyperbole, from the days when awed travellers such as Marco Polo brought home tales of its fabulous wealth and sophistication, but it has always lived up to its legendary inscrutability. The chances are, though, that the truth, as with all things, lies somewhere between the wildly positive and the wildly negative.

For outsiders, China has always been something of an enigma. Western observers are so used to a picture of society on a continual upward trajectory of science and technology, wealth and political freedom that they cannot quite understand a society that works any other way. This view of forward motion is so deep-rooted that the achievements or capabilities of earlier civilisations are often underestimated or downplayed, even in the West. China has never fitted into this pattern. A thousand years ago China reached a level of sophistication with its efficient Confucian government and its remarkable scientific and technological achievements that were way ahead of Europe. Then it was as if time in China stood still while Europe raced past, leaving China a backward, largely peasant society, described by

Karl Marx as 'a rotting semi-civilisation, vegetating in the teeth of time'.

So what has happened to put China back in the race, and running so strongly that it could overtake the West economically, and maybe even technologically? In the West, the current consensus is that political freedom and capitalist dynamics are the only recipe for genuine economic progress and a prosperous society, by allowing unfettered opportunities for trade and individual expression. That view was confirmed by the collapse of the Soviet Union, and the growing success of many of its former satellites. Yet China's growing prosperity seems to have been engineered by a government that is not simply authoritarian, but communist in its basic philosophy. This is such a conundrum that many western observers are convinced that China's future has to become increasingly capitalist and democratic if its economic engine is to keep running. Without those basic freedoms, these observers are certain the well of growth will soon run dry. Many also believe that as Chinese people acquire more and more of a taste for prosperity and what it can bring, the drive towards democratic capitalism will be unstoppable. However, this is far from the stated view of the Chinese leadership who believe they are on a firmly socialist road; it's just a special Chinese brand, described as 'socialism with Chinese characteristics'.

Go out into the west of China, into the hills of Sichuan, or the far reaches of the Yellow River, and you find a rustic China that is ancient and unchanging, with poor peasants working in paddy fields as they have done for thousands of years. Go to the cities of the east, however, and you see an urban landscape that is changing by the day, as old buildings are pulled down and new skyscrapers go up, and where young people are experiencing a lifestyle that is being transformed by both the arrival of western consumer technology and the buzz of their own ideas. Which one will be the future of China, new or old, communist or capitalist, authoritarian or democratic is still very much in the balance.

CHAPTER 1   CHINA'S BOOMING ECONOMY

'Socialism means eliminating poverty. Pauperism is not social-ism, still less communism ... To be rich is glorious.'
**Deng Xiaoping (1904–97), Paramount Leader
of the People's Republic of China**

In March 2007, the 3,000 delegates to China's National People's Congress (NPC) passed a law that might seem astonishing in what is usually described as a communist country. This new law, which is now enshrined in China's constitution, gives individuals the same legal protection for their property as the state. Of course, the law will make little difference to China's peasants who only hold their land on a short lease from the state and may make little actual difference to the country's growing army of middle-class home-owners who buy into 70-year state leases. But the implication of the new property ruling is clear – private property is fine, and must be protected by law.

Most western economists agree that making property rights enforceable is vital if China's amazing economic boom is to be sustained. There is little incentive to work and invest if you cannot be sure you will be able to hold on to the fruits of your investment. But, of course, private property is anathema to traditional communists. No wonder, then, that when it was first proposed in the Party in 2006, it was met with howls of protest from the leftists who saw it as the final straw of many sell-outs of communist ideals by China's reformist leaders. That the leadership carried the day – or that it was even thought of at all – is a testament not only to the degree of control the economic reformists in China's leadership now have but also to the astonishing momentum of the economic boom, which seems to be carrying all before it, and seems to render the arguments of its opponents ineffective.

The pace of China's economic progress has indeed been staggering. By the end of 2006, China will have achieved 28 years of rapid economic growth, averaging not far short of 10 per cent each year. This sustained rapid growth is impressive in itself, but what makes it that much more astonishing is its sheer scale. Between 1962 and 1989, Taiwan grew almost as fast, and between 1967 and 1993, so did Singapore. But these two economies are small compared with that of China. China's is massive. In 2006, China overtook the UK to become the world's fourth largest economy, outmoneyed only by the USA, Japan and Germany. Indeed, between 2001 and 2005, it accounted for a third of all global economic growth. Since

2000, China's contribution has been twice as large as the next three biggest emerging economies – India, Brazil and Russia – put together. What's more, unlike the Asian tigers of the 1960s to 1980s, the Chinese economic expansion shows no signs of slowing down. Many people confidently predict that it could outstrip even the USA within the next few decades to become the world's biggest economy.

How big is it?

There are some doubts about just how big the Chinese boom is. When China overtook the UK in 2006, it was partly because China's way of calculating its gross domestic product (GDP) changed. In 2005, the Chinese discovered an additional 17 per cent of economic output, in telecommunications, retailing

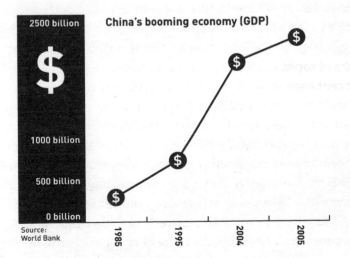

China's booming economy (GDP)

2500 billion

1000 billion

500 billion

0 billion

Source: World Bank

1985   1995   2004   2005

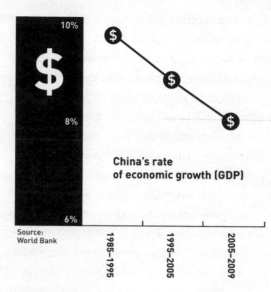

China's rate
of economic growth (GDP)

Source:
World Bank

10%

8%

6%

1985–1995

1995–2005

2005–2009

and property, that they had not previously included in their figures. The effect was to push China's 2004 figure for GDP above Italy (then sixth largest), and the following year above France and then the UK.

Chinese figures are almost certainly fudged in some ways. In the past, officials probably over-egged them to show what a good job they were doing. Now that the leadership is redirecting funds away from the booming east to poorer regions in the west of the country, there is instead a temptation to underestimate the figures. Thriving eastern regions fudge their figures downwards so they don't lose so much of their funding. Depressed western regions nudge them downwards, too, to prove how deserving of extra funding they are. Just how frustrated the leadership is by this manipulation is indicated by the fact that in 2003 it prosecuted for fraud 20,000 of the officials who produced them.

Even if the officials are meticulously straight, they can only work with the figures given to them by enterprises, which are notorious for double book-keeping and other ways of bending the figures. Beyond that, there is a huge underground economy involving unlicensed or even illegal businesses. So all in all it seems highly likely that the official figures for the size of China's economy are well below the reality.

There is another way, too, in which China's economy could be underestimated. It's a question of just what China's money will buy. For a long time now, China has pegged its currency the yuan (also known as the renminbi) rigidly to the US dollar, rather than letting it float up and down against it as other currencies do. So determined is China to keep this level pegging that it is prepared to spend a great deal of its massive foreign-currency reserves to keep the dollar and the yuan on track. It may be that if the yuan had not gone down against world currencies in recent years with the dollar, its economy would seem markedly bigger.

What the yuan will buy

In 2001, Jim Neill of the investment bank Goldman Sachs pointed out that China's economy might also turn out to be much larger if you looked at just what a dollar will buy in China. Some goods, such as oil, cost much the same almost anywhere in the world. But the cost of other goods such as food, rent and locally made consumer products vary tremendously. What will cost you US$5 in New York, you can often buy for little more than a dollar in China. So some economists prefer to use a system called purchasing power parity (PPP) to compare economies. On this basis, O'Neill showed, China accounted for 12.5 per cent of the world economy even back in 2001, and was already the world's second largest economy, just a little way behind the USA.

Not everyone agrees that PPP is a valid comparison, but it certainly backs up the case that China's economy is not just big, but may be even bigger than the official figures suggest. A couple of years after Neill's report, Goldman Sachs produced another report, this time making projections into the future. On this basis, the authors suggested, China is going to get so much bigger that even by conventional standards it will overtake Germany to become the world's third largest economy by 2010, Japan by 2016 and the USA by 2041, by which time its economy would be growing at a mere 3.5 per cent.

China's secret

So just how has China done it? How has one of the poorest, most backward countries in the world turned into such an economic powerhouse in such a short space of time?

The simplest and most complete reason is manpower. China has the world's biggest population, and the world's biggest labour force. In some ways, the vast Chinese workforce could be described as the world's most valuable resource. China may not have a wealth of natural resources, but it has hands to work by the billion, and the key to China's rise has been – and will be in the future – this vast labour force. It is not simply the numbers, though – staggering though they are. What is crucial is the huge number of 'floating' workers – the two hundred million or so migrant workers who have flooded into the urban areas from the country whenever needed to provide the sweat and toil that has kept factories going and built everything from apartment blocks to Olympic stadiums. Without these willing workers, often neglected and undervalued (see pages 75–88) but ever on tap, China's economic miracle would never have happened. In Shenzhen in the south, the place where it all started, migrant workers form 85 per cent of the city's ten million population.

The second reason is investment. The sums invested by the Chinese government in pushing the country forward are huge, and with so many taxpayers, they can be. But there is also plenty of foreign investment. Lured in by both the vast labour force and the potentially gigantic market, foreign investors have poured over US$50 billion a year into China – ten times as much as into India. Indeed, in 2002, China overtook the USA to become the world's biggest recipient of foreign money. The USA has since regained the lead, but the chances are it won't stay there for long. A lot of the money has come from Hong Kong and Taiwan, so isn't strictly speaking foreign, but the impact is the same. Money has poured in to get factories off the ground, to get cities rebuilt, to get businesses going – and the labour force has been there to turn the money into real economic progress and profit.

The Mao years

None of this would have happened, though, if it hadn't been for the revolution in the Chinese leadership's economic policy. It all began with the disaster of Mao Zedong's Great Leap Forward of 1958–61, which had promised China's rapid jump into a prosperous future. In fact, it brought nothing but catastrophe as the move to complete collective farming brought an agricultural downturn so appalling that between thirty and forty million Chinese people died from the resulting famine. Industry did little better, as over 98 per cent of industrial projects were stillborn. Even Mao had to admit the plan had failed and resigned as chairman of the People's Republic. Deng Xiaoping was among the Communist Party leaders to advocate a more pragmatic, less dogmatic approach, which allowed individual enterprise a little more room. With the aid of economist Chen Yun, Liu Shaoqi, who replaced Mao as chairman, shifted the balance of the Communist Party's economic strategy to allow individual farmers just a little more freedom to farm in their own way and to ensure that industries were run by managers, not bureaucrats.

As agricultural output recovered, and industry began to make headway, the Chinese economy began to look a little rosier in the 1960s. Mao, though, wasn't done, returning with a vengeance, literally, with his Great Proletarian Cultural Revolution (see pages 250–1). Liu was driven to an early grave. Deng was paraded round the streets of Beijing wearing a dunce's cap. And the Red Guard formed by young people with Mao's encouragement ravaged every city and village in their attacks on anything that could be called culture. Hundreds of thousands of China's brightest minds were killed or driven into exile. Once more the economy stagnated.

Deng's comeback

When Mao died in 1976, Deng Xiaoping gradually clawed his way back into power, despite the efforts of the infamous Gang of Four (see pages 251-2) to prevent it and, with Chen Yun, devised a new strategy. One key facet of Deng and Chen's new approach was to allow the collective farms to be broken up from 1978. Farms were leased back to individual farmers, who could plant what they liked and sell on the surplus (see pages 99-100). The results were better than anyone could have expected. With China's farmers at last in control of their own work, grain production rose by a third between 1978 and 1984, and the quantity and variety of Chinese farm produce swelled dramatically. With the cash they earned from their surplus production, farmers were even able to start up their own small sideline enterprises. In just seven years, the average income of rural households in China trebled.

Although the uplift in rural prosperity later stalled, the boost to farming not only gave China a larder full of food for the first time and a countryside full of people with a little cash to spare, it also freed up a huge number of people previously tied, needlessly, to working on the land. This was the real turning point.

Opening the door

The other key element of Deng's strategy was to instigate an 'open door' strategy. Under Mao, China's trade with the rest of the world had been almost non-existent. Deng argued that if China was to prosper, it had to begin to interact with foreign countries. 'If we isolate ourselves and close our doors again,' he said in 1978, 'it will be absolutely impossible for us to approach the level of the developed countries in fifty years.' His new open-door strategy was embodied in Special Economic Zones (SEZs) in which commercial tax rates would be halved and import duties would be waived altogether.

Three of the first four SEZs – Shenzhen, Zhuhai and Shantou – were in Guangdong, as near as possible to Hong Kong, and Hong Kong businessmen didn't miss a moment to step in and take advantage of the opportunities being landed at their feet. For the Hong Kong manufacturers it made eminent sense. Average factory wages in Hong Kong were US$4 an hour in 1990; in Guangdong, they were barely 50 cents. Not surprisingly, the factories went to Guangdong. By 1991, twenty-five thousand Hong Kongers had factories in Guangdong, employing three million people.

These changes set off an explosion in foreign trade. In 1985, Guangdong's exports were just US$2.9 billion; by 1994 they were over US$50 billion. As early as the mid-1980s, Guangdong had roared past Shanghai to become China's biggest foreign trader, and by the early 1990s Guangdong accounted for 40 per cent of all China's exports. The effect on Shenzhen in particular was astonishing. Within just a few years, Shenzhen was transformed from a small fishing port with a population of barely seventy thousand into a booming industrial city.

Not surprisingly, other regions wanted to get in on the act. In 1982, 14 other coastal towns were given a similar status to the SEZs, and then a year later a handful of regions were made 'open economic regions' including the Pearl River delta.

Stalling

However, all was far from rosy. The changes in the way state enterprises were run (see pages 43–44) meant that they began to hand over less and less of their earnings to the state. At the same time, the state began to spend heavily on direct investment and to hand out wads of cash to the enterprises in the form of state bank loans. Something would have to give soon. At the same time, farm production, after peaking in 1984, declined in the late 1980s, so the state had to pump in more and more cash to keep prices steady as its plan required. The same was true in industry, and it was a recipe for corruption. State enterprises and individuals would buy things at the state planned price, and then sell them on at twice the price on the black market.

Deng realized that, to start with, the planned prices would have to go, and prices would have to be freed up to float nearer their real market price. Unfortunately, he announced this idea before putting it into action. The result was chaos, with a wave of panic buying as everyone tried to get in while the state prices were still in place. Deng went ahead with the price liberalisation, but by then supplies were so short and hoarding so rife that inflation ran rampant. By the end of 1988, this was so out of hand that price controls were reimposed, and Deng had to take a back seat as a group of hardliners introduced a series of austerity measures.

It was against this background, with economic progress stalling and Deng's market reforms in reverse that China drew world attention to itself in the worst possible way, with the Tiananmen Square massacre (see pages 63–66). Ironically, this scared Chinese people so much that the government was able to carry out its austerity programme without even a whisper of dissent, with state loans cut by almost two-thirds and wages held right down. At the same time, farm production began to creep up. The combination of restricted money supply and extra production brought inflation back under control. Even price controls were quitely relaxed. Meanwhile, although the confidence of some foreign investors in China had wobbled after Tiananmen, Hong Kong manufacturers were already too deeply involved to hold back, and Guangdong's trading bubble was still swelling.

Deng goes south

As hardliners and reformers battled over the direction of China's economy, over the other side of the world, the Soviet Union was collapsing, and the Chinese leaders could not fail to see the people of Eastern Europe rejoicing as their great communist sidekick bit the dust. Deng was convinced that the only way for China's socialist future to survive was to push the reforms further. So, early in 1992, Deng set off on a special train to the south for what became known as his *Nan Xun* or Southern Tour. On 19 January, he arrived at Shenzhen's newly completed station, and immediately began to expound his strategy. Deng's tour was neither endorsed by the Party leadership nor even known about. This was a risky move by Deng, by then an incredible 87 years old, to seize the initiative and set the agenda – and it worked.

Deng's whole aim was to push the whole economic reform process further just when it was faltering. As he went on his four-day tour of the south, he hammered home his message that 'if the economy cannot be boosted ... [it] will only lead to a collapse and disintegration of the Communist Party'. To those critics who charged him with abandoning the spirit of communism, Deng argued forcefully that making money was not at odds with a socialist way of life. He urged local officials to be bold in pushing through further reforms and not act like 'a woman with bound feet'.

By choosing Shenzhen for his stand, Deng was not simply choosing a place where the eyes of the world would be upon him but a place that better than anything demonstrated the extraordinary effects the open door policy was having. Over the previous decade, Shenzhen's economy had gone grown by 50 per cent each year, and was, by 1991, worth an astonishing US$3.5 billion. Skyscrapers were shooting up on every corner and Shenzhen builders were able to demonstrate their reputation for adding three complete floors a day as they raced upwards. As Deng spoke, the message relayed on TV was unmistakable: China's reform works.

Open wide, please

Of course, Deng's strategy paid off and, by October, the National Party Congress was declaring that China had a 'socialist market economy'. Soon every city in China wanted a slice of the Shenzhen action. When Deng went on his Shenzhen trip in January 1992, there were just a hundred foreign investment zones. By the end of the year, there were 8,700. The Special Economic Zones Office (SEZO) wanted to organise them on the basis of the 'three alongs' – along the coast, along the Yangtze and along the border in the north-east. What SEZO said came to matter little, as provincial governments went ahead and announced their own. Hard on the heels of this development-zone mania came frenzied investment in the stock market and property.

In December 1992, the *Economist* issued a sixteen-page special on China entitled 'The Titan Stirs', drawing attention to China's rising economic might. The following year, David Roche and Barton Biggs of Morgan Stanley investment bank, both big wheels in the money markets, decided to go to China to see what all the fuss was about – and they were bowled over. In a report entitled excitedly 'China!', Biggs wrote, 'After eight days in China, I'm tuned in, overfed and maximum bullish.' China, he enthused, would be 'the mother of all bull markets'. The frenzied investment in the Hong Kong market that followed was dubbed *chao gupiao* or 'stir-fried stocks' so hot and sizzling was it. Biggs was so stunned by this China fever that he became worried that 'the craziness content about the magic of China is beginning to look like a bubble'. When other analysts underlined the doubts, Morgan Stanley decided to cut its Hong Kong holdings by a third. Immediately, the Hong Kong market slipped and many investors lost a lot of money.

Breaking China

It was just a temporary blip, however, and soon everyone was rushing to China as if to the January sales to see what they could get. In November 1993, German chancellor Helmut Kohl headed for Beijing accompanied by a glitzy entourage of Germany's biggest business leaders, including the heads of Siemens, Volkswagen–Audi and BMW. When Kohl came back gleefully waving contracts worth US$4.1 billion, including six Airbuses and a brand new metro system for Guangzhou, the scene was set for a stream of trade delegations from the world's richest nations. American secretary of commerce Ron Brown, British trade minister Michael Heseltine and French premier Edouard Balladur all came here, as did the heads of

China's changing economic base. Sectors (% of GDP)

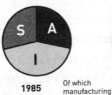

1985 Of which manufacturing 34.9%   1995   2004

A = Agriculture   I = Industry   S = Services

Source:
World Bank

CHINA TECH

It's often assumed that China's products are bottom-end cheap-and-cheerful items like toys and clothes. It's certainly true that they do this kind of thing very well, but China's recent economic boom has been driven by much more sophisticated products. In fact, a third of all China's exports are categorised as high technology. Indeed, in 2004 China's exports of information and communication technology – mobile phones, laptops, digital cameras and so on – exceeded those of the USA by quite a substantial margin, reaching US$180 billion compared with the USA's $149 billion. That was the year, too, when the Chinese firm Lenovo took over IBM's personal computer division. All the signs are that China's high-tech business will grow and grow. It has always been seen simply as a factory floor for putting western ideas and designs into practice at low cost. But that may be beginning to change. China has as yet not a single identifiable brand name to compete with those of the major western and Japanese companies, but there is a vast new generation of technology graduates emerging from China's education system, and keen to put their ideas into practice. Most of them are likely to go to foreign-owned firms where they get the best access to western technology and ideas, but it may be that they will soon put their skills into practice with home-grown companies.

nearly every major multinational, from General Motors (GM) to Coca-Cola. In little more than two years, from the end of 1993 to the beginning of 1996, trips such as this yielded contracts worth US$40 billion or more.

Many of the promises took surprisingly long to come through, but such was the confidence inspired by the size and the cheapness of the Chinese workforce and the prospects of the Chinese market that most investors stuck with it, even through the 1997 Asian economic downturn. Such were the future vistas of profit that big multinationals such as GM were prepared to jump through hoops and invest an enormous amount of money in simply getting the licence to operate in China from the Chinese government, which played notoriously hard to get. China 'experts' such as Henry Kissinger and George Bush Senior made small fortunes going on PR trips for companies trying to get deals secured. Until recently, foreign multinationals were not allowed to run their own businesses in China but had to go into partnership with a Chinese enterprise. Yet the trouble of finding the right partner and figuring out how to work with them is something that countless foreign companies thought worth while.

Trading up

There is no doubt that China's trading door has been opened wider to the world than anyone could have imagined thirty years ago. When Deng's open-door policy first began, China was effectively a closed economy, buying in virtually nothing from the outside world and selling nothing either. Combined exports and imports accounted for less than 10 per cent of the country's GDP. Within a decade they were worth 30 per cent of GDP, and by 2002, they were worth half of all China's GDP. Since China's economy had grown by near enough 10 per cent a year for all that period, that amounted to a huge stride into the world economy. In 1978, China accounted for just 0.6 per cent of all world trade. By the time China was admitted into the World Trade Organization in 2001, it accounted for over 5 per cent. In 2004, it outstripped Japan, the world's postwar economic miracle, as the world's third largest exporter, with exports worth US$593 billion, compared with Japan's US$565 billion. Only the USA (US$819 billion) and Germany (US$915 billion) exported more.

The China price

There's no doubt that the sudden and dramatic arrival of China on the world economic stage has had a huge impact elsewhere. In his book *China Inc* (2006), Ted Fishmann explains how in 2003 a report by the Chicago Federal Reserve Bank described how American automotive-parts makers were complaining that car makers had been asking them for 'the China price' on their purchases. What they meant by 'the China price' was the lowest price possible, since whatever price you could make something for, the Chinese were almost certain to be able to make it substantially cheaper. *Business Week* described how 'In general, [the China price] means 30 to 50 per cent less than what you can possibly make something for in the US. In the worst cases it means below the cost of your materials. Makers of apparel, footwear, electric appliances, and plastic products, which have been shutting US factories for decades, know well the futility of trying to match the China price' (quoted in David Smith's *The Dragon and the Elephant* (2007)). This kind of thinking has fuelled the idea that the only way for some companies to survive is to move at least some of their business to China.

If the China price is worrying for manufacturers, it is even more worrying for their employees. Even in the best-case scenario when your company keeps its factory in the western world going, the China price severely undermines your bargaining power for wages. While those at the top of the tree are doing well because of the dramatic expansion of world trade, those further down have found their wages falling behind. In the worst-case scenario, your company closes down and moves all its operations to China, or simply goes out of business. A poll of America's manufacturing workforce revealed that a third of them fear they are going to lose their jobs to overseas competition. And they are right to worry. Since the turn of the twenty-first century, America's manufacturing sector has been haemorrhaging jobs like never before. Between 2000 and 2003, the USA lost nearly three million jobs in manufacturing.

For those lucky enough to hang on to their jobs and maintain their wages, the China price has been a real boon. The price of products like clothing, shoes and electronic gadgets has tumbled. Things like DVDs, which were once big occasional purchases, can now be impulse buys for almost anyone in the rich countries. Even personal computers have come way down in price.

Chinese shoppers stick

If the impact of the vast Chinese labour force has been marked, its fabled giant market has been less so. One of the reasons is that despite its giant economy, its population is so vast that the average income of its people is still pretty low. China's gross national income (GNI) is just US$1,740 per capita, or less than US$5 a day. That's more than twice as good as India's, but it compares with US$37,600 per capita in the UK, and US$44,000 per capita in the USA. Even allowing for the fact that the dollar buys four or fives times as much of many items in China as it does in the USA that still means the average Chinese person has still very little to spend. And, of course, what they do have, they're not inclined to spend anyway.

The Chinese, especially the older generation, are the world's biggest savers, with more than one–and-a-quarter trillion dollars of savings even on conservative estimates. Unlike people in the western economies, who are happy to borrow and spend, keeping the consumer market rattling along, the Chinese put any spare money away for a rainy day and rarely, if ever, borrow for personal spending. The Chinese have always been a prudent people, and with the widespread poverty, and the traumatic memories of very hard times fresh in the memory, it is hardly surprising if they are especially cautious now. With the taking away of China's welfare safety net in recent years, most people know they need to save for

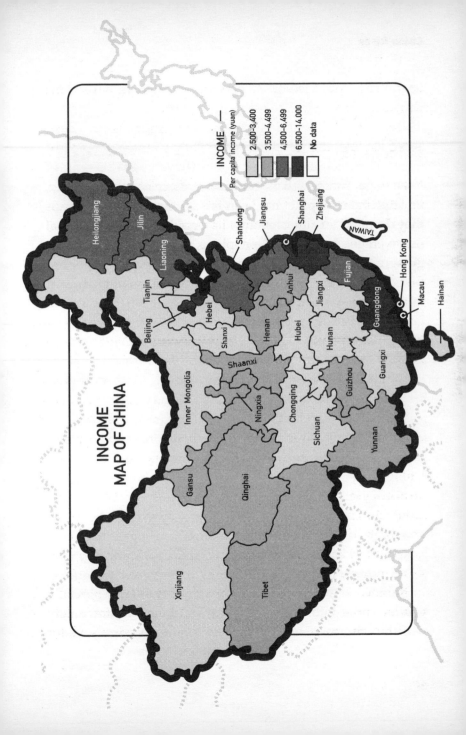

INCOME MAP OF CHINA

INCOME
Per capita income (yuan)

2,500–3,400
3,500–4,499
4,500–6,499
6,500–14,000
No data

Heilongjiang
Jilin
Liaoning
Shandong
Jiangsu
Shanghai
Zhejiang
TAIWAN
Tianjin
Beijing
Hebei
Anhui
Fujian
Hong Kong
Macau
Hainan
Shanxi
Henan
Hubei
Jiangxi
Hunan
Guangdong
Shaanxi
Inner Mongolia
Ningxia
Chongqing
Guizhou
Guangxi
Gansu
Qinghai
Sichuan
Yunnan
Xinjiang
Tibet

everything from medical emergencies to education for their children, all of which are now self-financed.

Moreover, although people in the western world worry about job loss, the fact that forty million Chinese people lost their jobs in manufacturing in the early years of this century – twice the total number of manufacturing jobs in the USA – must play on people's minds, especially as there is no unemployment benefit. The changes in China's economy mean that many people are losing their jobs as they get older, too, and older can often mean simply over the age of 40. With the pension cushion gone, as well, it makes a lot of sense to hang on to your money and not get into debt.

BEST CHINA

In July 2007, a row seemed to be coming to a head between China and the USA over product quality and safety. Over the previous few months, a number of products from China had come under critical scrutiny in America, including tainted or defective toothpaste, tyres, toys and fish. Some politicians began to call for pressure on American companies that fail to make the appropriate quality checks on products from China in their quest for ever cheaper imports and higher profits. Some, though, pointed the finger firmly at China and its lack of regulation in factories. The Chinese immediately retaliated with a ban on American food products believed to be linked to disease outbreaks. Whatever the outcome of this dispute, the question over the quality of Chinese factories is unlikely to go away. It is not only the quality of the products that causes concern – especially with the toys that China makes so many of – but the safety of workers. There is no doubt that many Chinese factory owners do cut corners on both quality and safety to undercut competition and meet deadlines, but it is hard to say just how widespread the problems are. Occasionally some horrific instances of workers being exposed to very dangerous working conditions or working inhuman hours for little pay do come to light. Occasionally, too, some terrible reports of child labour come to light. But it is hard to tell if these are common or very rare. One thing that human-rights campaigners say is that if these abuses are widespread it is the responsibility of foreign companies that buy in China as much as the Chinese businesses themselves. They may be able to turn a blind eye to what is going on, but it is their pressure to cut costs further and further and respond to impossible deadlines that is helping fuel these abuses.

Spending in Beijing

The leadership, though, are all too aware of the dragging effect this money hoarding is having on the economy. In March 2006, Prime Minister Wen Jiabao told the National People's Congress that he would find some way of releasing China's pent-up cash. Acknowledging the worries about the future, he said, 'We will address people's concerns that increasing consumption will make them unable to meet basic living standards.'

Yet although Mr Wen is going to have to work at getting most Chinese people to part with their cash, some need no persuasion. Young and reasonably well-to-do urbanites are fuelling a consumer spending boom in the cities. They might be proportionally a small part of the Chinese population, but there are still enough of them to create a substantial market. In its 2005 report on China, the Organisation for Economic Co-operation and Development (OECD) referred to statistics that showed that for every 100 Chinese households there are 46 refrigerators, 94 colour TVs, 12 personal computers, 28 air conditioners and 59 washing machines. With hundreds of millions of households in China, that's a pretty big market for items like these.

There's also a growing market in the cities for luxury items. The China Association of Branding Strategy says that 175 million Chinese people had incomes over US$30,000 a year in 2005 and could afford at least some indulgences. An Ernst and Young report the same year predicted that sales of luxury goods in China would swell by 20 per cent every year between 2005 and 2008, then 10 per cent a year until 2015. If Ernst and Young are right, then in less than a decade, China will become the world's biggest market for luxury goods, accounting for a third of global demand. When it comes to choosing what to buy, foreign brands still have a cachet in China that the country's home-grown brands can't yet match. The young urbanites tend to buy German cars, Japanese electronics, and European fashion and cosmetics such as Chanel,

Prada and Gucci. So all these brands will surely be hot-footing it to China in order to make the most of the opportunities.

China's poor

Those young urbanites on US$30,000, however numerous, are the exception. Most Chinese people earn much, much less. Indeed, the average wage in China is barely US$1,500, and many take home considerably less. Poverty is particularly acute in the countryside where 800 million people earn on average a third of what Chinese people earn in cities. And 26 million people in rural China live in what is called 'absolute poverty', which officially means earning less than a dollar a day but in reality is a state of destitution so utter that they don't even have a bed for the night and enough food to eat.

Yet although China's people are far from well off, very few now suffer the kind of abject poverty that is often seen in India and Africa. After the disasters of the Mao years, China has succeeded in alleviating poverty better than anywhere else in the world. Indeed, since the reforms started in the 1978, 400 million people have been lifted out of poverty. What's more, the number of people living in absolute poverty has been cut 90 per cent, from 250 million in 1980 to 26 million today. The number of people around the world living in absolute poverty fell in the 1990s from 1.29 to 1.17 billion, but if it hadn't been for the dramatic reduction in China, the number would actually have gone up. It wasn't just in monetary terms that China improved life for the poor, either. The United Nation's human-development index ranked China 85th in the world out of 177. While China was still a poor country in terms of income, it had the high level of literacy and life expectancy associated with middle-income countries like those of Eastern Europe.

It is an extraordinary achievement. Paul Wolfowitz, former head of the World Bank, whose name was in the headlines when he was forced out of his job for personal misconduct, was a keen observer of international economies. When Wolfowitz visited China in 2005, he observed, 'East Asia has experienced the greatest increase in wealth for the largest number of people in the shortest time in the history of mankind.'

There is no doubt that this reduction in poverty is in large part due to China's move into the global market, which has brought money flooding into the country. However, the gradual reduction in poverty is beginning to stall, especially in the countryside (see pages 100–102), and the gap between rich and poor is starting to open up as some people are left behind in the race to, in Deng's famous words, 'get rich first'. In the 1990s, the government took away state support for failing state enterprises, and for state housing, education and health. It freed up money to invest in the country's future, reduced inefficiency and allowed individual enterprises to flourish, but it cut away the support for many vulnerable people, especially the old. The result is that China is now a more divided society in terms of wealth than even the USA.

PROFILE: DENG XIAOPING

When Deng Xiaoping died in 1997 at the age of 92, Time magazine, which had already twice named him man of the year, described him as 'the last emperor'. It was suitably contradictory praise. Deng is rightly credited as the man who initiated the reforms that made China a market economy and helped lift hundreds of millions of people out of poverty. At his funeral, President Jiang Zemin declared, 'The decision to take economic construction as the centre represents the most fundamental achievement under Comrade Deng Xiaoping's leadership, in the effort to bring order out of chaos.' Jiang was right, for it was Deng's leadership that took China out of the devastation of the Cultural Revolution and guided it on its road to economic progress. Yet Deng was also the man who supported Mao in his disastrous economic plans for the Great Leap Forward, and refused to let go of any of the power of the Communist Party over the lives of ordinary people. Most notoriously, it was Deng who was behind the brutal suppression of students in Tiananmen Square.

Deng was one of the original Chinese communists and it is his longevity that has helped give him lasting fame, for his greatest achievements didn't come until he was over 80. He was born in a village not far from Chongqing in 1904 as Deng Xiansheng, but went to study in France before returning to China to join Zhou Enlai's young communists in the 1920s. To mark the occasion he changed his name from Xiansheng to Xiaoping, which means 'Little Peace'. Although small, he was physically tough and played a key role in the Long March (see pages 243–4) and the civil war that finally brought the Communists to power in 1949. Deng soon came to play a key role in the leadership of the Party, especially in economic planning, but he frequently clashed with Mao. Deng thought Mao was outdated; Mao thought Deng was high-handed. While Mao was alive, Deng was continually being booted out, then making a comeback. It was only when Mao died in 1976 that Deng was able to consolidate his position as China's leader – though even then he had to make a comeback from a purge by the Gang of Four (see pages 251–2) that was led by Mao's widow.

From the late 1970s on, when Deng was clearly in charge, he introduced a raft of reforms including letting peasants farm family plots and the growth of hybrid enterprises. He also led the way to opening China up to foreign trade and investment with the creation of the Special Economic Zones in the south, which soon became the engines of China's economic boom. By the time he retired from the scene in the mid-1990s, China's dramatic move towards a market economy was well under way, but he also helped to ensure that the Communist government was as authoritarian in its outlook as ever.

Donning the red hat

One of the reasons for this widening wealth gap is the little heralded but dramatic change in the way businesses are run in China. The changes have given Chinese entrepreneurs the chance to spread their wings and help bring China its new-found wealth, but they've also helped concentrate that wealth into fewer hands.

It all began in the city of Wenzhou on the east coast about a quarter of a century ago. Wenzhou, in those days, was pretty isolated from the rest of China, without a railway and surrounded by mountains only traversed by unpaved roads. A local ditty went '*Qiche tiao, Wenzhou dao*' – 'When your vehicle jumps, you're on the way to Wenzhou'. This very isolation, though, was why China's business revolution started here, far away from the prying eyes of Beijing, a vital requirement since it was all highly illegal.

Once Mao's collectives started to break up and individual households were allowed to go into business with township and village enterprises after 1978 (see pages 99–100), the people of Wenzhou seized the chance with both hands. In every village in Wenzhou, families set up their own small businesses. In some villages, nine out of ten households did. In just six years, a hundred thousand businesses like this appeared; in nine years there were a hundred and ninety thousand of them. They all began as very small businesses, typically what the Chinese call '*qian dian, hou chang*' ('shop in front, factory behind') – each mini-factories for consumer goods such as pens, cigarette lighters, shoes and clothes.

The problem was they were not legally allowed to expand. The law forbade them from 'exploiting' more than five workers, and also from raising money for expansion. So the enterprising people of Wenzhou found all kinds of ingenious ways round these problems. They set up 'stockholding co-operatives', which sounded very socialist and like the state collectives, which could employ any number of people. In reality, they were just private businesses that kept their socialist credentials by giving a quarter of their profits to their employees. Another wheeze was to set up 'hang-on household enterprises', in which a household business pretended to be an offshoot of a state-owned enterprise, so that it could not only raise loans but also escape tax. Most of these ruses worked a treat, and Wenzhou's pirate factories helped multiply the income of the city six-fold in just twelve years. Yet Wenzhou officials were so nervous about Beijing's reaction to these semi-legal activities that when they recorded the rising output, they put it down as 'collective' activity, so that it all seemed like an amazing display of socialist ideas at work. In Wenzhou, they called this *dai hong maozi* ('donning the red hat') and these hybrid businesses came to be called 'red-hat' businesses.

Crossing the river

Gradually the whole idea of red-hat businesses spread across the country and the government allowed them to spread. Just as Deng got the inspiration for letting farmers farm their own land from the illegal activities of eighteen renegades (see pages 99–100), so the red-hats and town and village enterprises showed the leadership how private business might work in a socialist country. It was, as Deng acknowledged, all rather a shock. 'It was as if a strange army appeared in the countryside making and selling a huge variety of products,' he said in 1987. 'This is not the achievement of our central government ... This was not something I thought of ... This was a surprise.' As Deng famously said, China had to 'cross the river by feeling the stones'.

The problem is that the legal status of these hybrid businesses is often far from certain. They take a huge variety of forms and there is still a lot of argument about how they fit into socialist industrial structures. Of course, operating on the fringes like this has hugely coloured the way Chinese people do business. To make the system work, Chinese businessmen have to be skilful at playing the system as well as good at business, and ready to bend the rules with bribes, secret deals and the special Chinese form of networking called *guanxi* (see page 66). Foreigners doing business in China, or competing with Chinese businesses, often find the cloak of secrecy, the networking and the often scant regard for legalities deeply maddening, but this is the way the Chinese have had to work to get businesses working in what remains a socialist country.

State business

The very success of the red-hat businesses and small-scale township and village enterprises (see pages 99–100) created a real problem for the leadership for it highlighted just how hopelessly inefficient the big state-owned enterprises (SOEs) were.

Up until the mid-1990s, pretty much half the urban workforce – over a hundred million people – worked in the state-run factories, which made everything from cycles to chopsticks. Many of these SOEs in Shanghai in particular were former private factories that had been nationalised after the revolution. Others, especially in the north, were factories set up in the first wave of communism in the 1950s, including much of China's heavy industry – its oil refineries, its steel works and its coal mines. The SOEs were very different from the UK's nationalised industries. In the UK, nationalised industries like the NHS simply employ workers for a wage. Chinese SOEs were a welfare state in themselves, providing health care, education for workers, children, accommodation and even pensions. Indeed, people could spend their whole lives in an SOE, from the cradle to the grave. Often workers could even pass jobs on to their children.

The support and security meant that jobs in an SOE were highly coveted. They provided the linchpin of social stability in Chinese cities throughout the second half of the twentieth century, and in some ways that was their most important function. The problem was that, as the hybrid businesses revealed all too clearly, they were often hopelessly inefficient. Output was invariably low and raw materials, energy and labour were wasted on a gargantuan scale.

After the success of the hybrids, the Chinese government began to realise they had to make the SOEs stand on their own feet as businesses. It tried various measures to get things moving. It set up new stock exchanges in Shanghai and Shenzhen to try and attract investment. This worked for some of the bigger enterprises, but few people wanted to put their money in badly run businesses with a huge burden of social welfare responsibilities. Another scheme was to let managers retain a share of the profits to give them incentives for increased productivity, but since the SOEs bought raw material at state-controlled low prices this simply meant that the state paid to line the managers' pockets. A third idea was to amalgamate badly run SOEs with well-run ones to see if they would get on better together.

Thatcherism with Chinese characteristics

None of this worked, and eventually the government began to realise it would have to treat the SOEs as businesses. The man behind the reforms was Zhu Rhongji, China's deputy prime minister from 1993 to 1998 and prime minister from 1998 to 2003. Mr Zhu was a great fan of Margaret Thatcher in Britain and had studied her privatisations in the 1980s with great interest. He became convinced that just as Mrs Thatcher had seen over the 'rationalisation' of the workforces in the British coal and steel industries, so he would have to slash the workforce in China's state enterprises. In future, China would have to rely on market forces and private enterprises to create new jobs. Many people believe Zhu Rhongji's push for China to join the World Trade Organization was in part motivated by the realisation that he might need the help of outside pressure to drive these reforms along.

The world has focused so much attention on China's economic miracle, that the devastating scale of Mr Zhu's reforms is often overlooked. Nearly forty thousand state-run businesses were shut down in just a few years, and between 1996 and 2001 a terrifying fifty-three million people lost their jobs. In many cities in the north, half the workforce was made redundant almost overnight. In his book *China Inc*, Ted Fishmann makes a telling comparison. The loss of jobs was significantly worse than if the world's five hundred biggest global corporations from Wal-Mart to Exxon suddenly shut down. Some enterprises kicked people out of their jobs but continued to give them welfare support – so were paying out, but getting no labour in return. With other enterprises, the redundant workers not only lost their jobs; they lost their homes, their children's education, their medical support and their pensions.

THE XIA GANG

The aim with the redundancies from the state-run businesses, the government said at the time, was to gradually push the xia gang (laid off) workers out into society and create a new social-welfare system separate from the workplace. Of course it is taking time to build in the support. In the meanwhile, tens of millions of Chinese people are struggling to get by. It has been especially hard for slightly older people, particularly women over the age of 40 who are finding it almost impossible to get work in factories or in the new service industries where employers unashamedly advertise for young, attractive, single women. The problem is that people in their 40s and 50s rarely have skills other than the basic skills they learned in the state factories, and because they come from the generation that was brought up during the Cultural Revolution they have little education either. In Shanghai, 4,050 units are being set up to find ways to get this generation back into work – but most of the work they find is in jobs like cleaning for the bright young urbanites, and so half a century on from the Communist Revolution, China is getting a servant class again.

Today, the Chinese private sector accounts for over half of Chinese industrial production. Foreign-owned businesses and joint ventures account for a good deal of the rest. Barely a fifth comes from entirely state-run businesses. Similarly, barely a fifth of China's non-farm workforce work in state industries. So the vast majority of China's businesses and workers must sink or swim in the market. Some call it market socialism, others call it 'socialism with Chinese characteristics' – and others say it is simply capitalism with a Chinese mask. Whatever it is, it is certainly changing China, and changing it rapidly.

CHAPTER 2   CHINA'S POLITICS

'We're going down an evil road. The whole country is at a most precarious time.'

Open letter from seventeen former top Communist Party officials and conservative academics, 16 July 2007

In July 2007, the letter from which the above quote is taken appeared on the Internet. Occasionally letters critical of China's leadership do appear on the Web, only to be quickly blocked, but most of these are from human-rights activists protesting about China's lack of liberties. This one, though, was unusual. It came not from liberals outside the Party, but from the other side, from conservatives within the Party and included former government ministers.

Their criticism was not that the Party had not opened up enough, but that it had opened up too much. The signatories of this letter were angry because they felt the party had gone too far down the path of economic liberalisation. They condemned the passing of the law allowing private property back in March 2007, which they felt was a betrayal of socialist principles that protected the fortunes of corrupt officials and the ill-gotten gains of crooked businesspeople. They wanted to reverse the move in 2002 to let private businesspeople join the Communist party. They wanted to restrict foreign investment. They wanted to end the privatisation of state assets. The Party is heading on a dangerous road towards capitalism, they claimed, and the wealth gap is growing. If China wasn't careful, it would soon have its own Boris Yeltsin, and then 'the demise of the party and country would loom'.

THE CHINESE COMMUNIST PARTY

With a membership of over 70 million, the Chinese Communist Party is the world's largest political party. Unlike Western political parties, the CCP is deeply involved in everyday life – overseeing what Chinese people learn at school and watch on TV, their jobs and homes, and even the size of their families. There is a party representative in every village keeping an eye on things. If a woman in a village gets pregnant, for instance, local party officials will often know as soon as she does. The influence of the party in rural areas has lessened in recent years, though, as farmers have been allowed more freedom to farm their own land as they choose. In urban areas, too, the party's influence has waned with the break-up of State-Owned Enterprises. As a result, people are not quite so desperate to join the party in order to get on in life as they once were, which may be one reason the party was opened up, controversially, to a wider membership a few years ago, including to private entrepreneurs.

All the same, joining the party does still bring significant privileges, which is why membership continues to rise. Members are kept in the know about what is going on in the country, they get to make crucial personal relationships, they can apply for jobs open only to party members (including key government posts) and their children get better schooling. Joining is far from easy, since it requires the sponsorship of several Party members, plus extensive vetting, then a year's probation and training. It's hardly surprising, then, that the CCP is far from representative, with women making up less than 20 per cent of party members, and with nearly 80 per cent of members over the age of 35.

The Communist Party usually likes to present a unified front, and settle its differences behind closed doors. This was probably the first time an internal Party dispute had been aired so visibly in public – though the website was blocked within a day. In itself, the letter is probably not that significant. In fact, it probably shows the signatories' desperation at not being heard, rather than their strength. Interestingly, it came hot on the heels of news, reported in *China Daily*, that three million private businesspeople had joined the Party since 2002. So the signatories may have felt walls were beginning to crack. The timing, however, was significant. Just a few months after this, two thousand party leaders were due to meet at the Party's National Congress.

CHINA'S PARTIES

Besides the CCP, there are eight officially recognised 'democratic' parties in China: the Chinese Nationalist Party, the China Democratic League, the China Democratic National Construction Association, the China Association for Promoting Democracy, the Chinese Peasants' and Workers' Democratic Party, the China Zhi Gong Dang, the Third September Society and the Taiwan Democratic Self-Government League. None of these parties, though, could be considered in any way an opposition to the CCP. They are very small, and only allowed to exist because the CCP permits them to. They were simply the parties who turned up to the CCP's invitation to their conference setting up the People's Republic in 1948 and agreed to accept the CCP's supervision. If they ever seriously opposed the CCP, they would be instantly stamped out. Nevertheless, individual democratic party members still do occasionally make progress to high office, such as Duanmu Zheng, who became vice-president of the Supreme Court in 1990.

The big party

The National Party Congress is a Party event, and is not to be confused with the National People's Congress, which is China's version of parliament. The Party Congress happens once every five years and is the most important event in Chinese politics. This is when the Party decides general policy direction for the next five years. It also decides the line-up for the Party's Central Committee, which in turn decides the line-up of the 24-man Politburo from which is selected the nine-man Politburo Standing Committee – basically the inner circle that makes all the big decisions and essentially runs China. All these tiers get chosen pretty simultaneously, so, above all, the Party Congress is the time when the Party decides who is in and who is out. Although the winners and losers are never announced publicly, you can tell who is doing well by the position of their photographs in the official Party newspaper, the *People's Daily*.

The previous Congress in 2002 saw a change of leadership right at the very top, when President Jiang Zemin stepped down as the Party's general secretary. The general secretary is both the official Party leader (prior to 1980, the chairman was leader) and usually now the president, too, and so is the most powerful man in China. In the early days of the People's Republic, power tended to come from personal influence rather than formal position, so Mao remained powerful even after he resigned as Party leader in 1962 and Deng Xiaoping was effectively in charge through the 1980s and early 1990s even though he held no official party posts. Gradually, however, the official position has become crucial. So when Jiang Zemin stepped down at the 2002 Congress to let Hu Jintao become both general secretary and president in 2003, it was a sea change in the leadership at the top – and perhaps the first formal and clear handover of power in the history of the People's Republic, although Jiang still continues to wield some influence. It spelled the end, too, for Jiang's premier, Zhu Rongji, since only one of Zhu's supporters, vice-premier Wen Jiabao, made it on to the Politburo Standing Committee, and within a year Zhu had gone too.

PROFILE: HU JINTAO

Even though Hu Jintao has been President of China for since 2003, in its most internationally active phase for some time, he remains a little-known figure around the world. When he first came to power, foreign journalists were describing him as a mystery man. *Newsweek* said, 'the most noteworthy thing about him was how little was known about him'. The *Chicago Tribune* suggested his anonymity might be deliberate in a kind of backhanded compliment: 'It has taken extraordinary skill to remain such a cipher.' Now he is better known, but remains something of an enigma, and what emerges is someone who believes in restraint and caution, and never being hasty. In his time as President, he has been a consensus builder, which may be why politically, he seems to fall between the liberals calling for an even more market-led economy, and the hardliners wanting to rein in the economic reforms and return to a purer form of socialism. Hu's stated vision is to build a 'harmonious society' by taking care to look after the poor and disadvantaged as well as creating wealth. The challenges he faces in achieving this goal are huge, which may be why he has been keen on developing an untroubled relationship with the world outside. He has devoted considerable effort to what some people call 'smile diplomacy' with China's neighbours – and has been instrumental in reducing some of the tensions with Japan.

Born in Jiangsu in 1942, Hu was a graduate in hydraulic engineering and came into the Party via the Youth League, which is where he draws most of his support. It was Deng who picked him in 1992, to be leader of the fourth generation, and ensured he became the second youngest ever member of the Politburo Standing Committee. It soon became clear that Hu would succeed Jiang Zemin as leader, but his fastidiously polite, courteous manner ensured he never ruffled Jiang's feathers, and his accession to power in 2003 was, as things go in China, smooth enough considering Jiang's reluctance to leave the stage. In a profile in the *New York Times*, Robert Zoellick comments, '[Hu's] greatest legacy may turn out to be selecting the leadership that will continue his domestic strategy while moving quickly to position China constructively in the world.'

Hu's harmonious society

The handover from Jiang Zemin and Zhu Rongji to Hu Jintao and Wen Jiabao, who became premier after Zhu, marked a change of direction for Chinese policy. Jiang and Zhu were determined followers of Deng's open-door, getting-rich-first approach, and went even further than Deng in encouraging open trade, foreign investment and the development of private enterprises. It was Jiang who campaigned for private businesspeople to be allowed to join the Party, and it was Zhu whose efforts finally saw China admitted to the World Trade Organization in 2001.

Hu and Wen, however, have been more cautious in their approach to the market. Hu has focused on the wealth gap that has opened up between the rich and poor as a result of the liberalisations and the dismantling of state support. The wealth gap has increased social tension and sparked a dramatic rise in social protest over such issues as land grabs (see pages 95–6). Hu's avowed aim is to reduce this tension by addressing such issues to create a 'harmonious society'. What this means in practice is shifting the focus away from economic growth and paying more attention to welfare support, especially in rural areas, and redirecting more of the development investment away from the booming coastal regions towards the struggling interior in the West.

The leadership changes at the 2007 Congress were not as dramatic as those back in 2002, since Hu Jintao will now remain president until the 2012 Congress, with Wen as premier alongside him. Nevertheless, there were telling promotions of this protégé's.

THE TIERS OF GOVERNMENT

There are four major tiers of government in China: national, provincial, prefectural and county. There are 23 provinces including Taiwan, plus 4 municipalities at the same level (Beijing, Shanghai, Chongqing and Xi'an) and five autonomous regions (Tibet, Xinjiang, Inner Mongolia, Guanxi and Ningsia), in which a slightly different form of government is extended to the non-Han people. Below the provinces are 300 prefectures and smaller municipalities, made up from 2500 or so counties.

Connections and factions

With no open debate and no political parties, China's government policies are driven very much by the personal choices of those at the top. So it is crucial for the leadership to surround itself with like-minded people, and jockeying for support is a key element in Chinese politics. Progress is by patronage and support comes from protégés. Before the Congress, President Hu will have been busy behind the scenes, sizing people up, making sure his chosen men are given the right jobs to strengthen his grip on power.

There are two distinct factions within the Party, however, leading to the kind of neat description so beloved by the Chinese of 'one party, two factions'. On the one side is the Shanghai coalition, made up largely of officials who have risen from the booming urban and coastal provinces. On the other is the *tuan pai*, the Communist Youth League faction, made up largely of officials who have come up from the Youth Leagues in the poorer rural interior. Some describe the Shanghai coalition as right-leaning and elitist and in favour of further market liberalisation while the Youth League are more populist and inclined to emphasise the need to boost welfare support for poorer rural districts. But it would be wrong to see both as simple political groupings in the western sense. They are based much more on personal interaction than unity of policies.

Hu Jintao's power base is in the Chinese Communist Youth League, and it is people who have come up through this that he is likely to favour. Late in 2006, Hu made a crucial move to reduce the influence of the Shanghai faction ahead of Party Congress year. The godfather of the Shanghai group is Jiang Zemin who, although no longer in power, still wields considerable influence behind the scenes. Hu couldn't go for Jiang, but instead he went for Chen Liangyu, the leader of the Shanghai branch of the Communist Party. While Hu was giving Jiang a lavish launch for his new book, Beijing investigators descended on Chen's Shanghai party office and exposed a corrupt deal involving the use of citizens' pension funds to pay for a dodgy property deal. As a result, Chen was sacked from all his party posts, and the power of the Shanghai faction was considerably weakened.

On the up

With Hu in the ascendant, it is likely that he will promote the interests of rising stars from his *tuan pai* power base such as Li Keqiang, whom some tip to be China's next president, and Li Yuanchao. In China, in a manner that is distinctly reminiscent of the Confucian respect for elders, the handover of power is very much on an age basis, so those holding the reins all tend to be much the same age. Jiang and Zhu were described as China's third generation of leaders, Hu and Wen, both in their 60s, are described as the fourth generation, and rising leaders like Li Keqiang and Li Yuanchao who, in their mid-40s to mid-50s, are the fifth generation.

PROFILE: LI KEQIANG

Born in 1955 in Dingyuan in the poor province of Anhui, Li Keqiang is one of the younger 'fifth generation' of politicians on the way up in Chinese politics. He came up through the Youth League, which is why he is connected to Hu Jintao, and in 1999 became China's youngest ever state governor when he took the leadership of Henan, the country's most heavily populated province. In 2004 he was given the top Party ranking in Liaoning province, as secretary of the Communist Party of China Liaoning Province Committee. Some sources describe him as outspoken with a sharp tongue, but Newsweek has described him as 'cautious and well-connected', and so careful in his preparation that apparently 'He memorises his speeches and doesn't make any mistakes'. This reliability is what perhaps recommends him to Hu Jintao, who, it is said, counts Li as one of his protégés, which is why at the 2007 Congress, Li joined the Politburo Standing Committee to become China's seventh most powerful man.

Because so many of China's power struggles go on behind closed doors, it is hard to be certain exactly how it all works. It is certainly different from western democratic governments. There are essentially three power bases in China – the Communist Party, the official government and the People's Liberation Army. In recent years, the power of the army has declined, even though the military budget has gone up, mainly because the army is no longer allowed to set up its own production enterprises to make equipment. So it's the Party and the official government which effectively run China.

The state of the party

There is no doubt that the Communist Party is in charge, but its relation with the official government is subtle and complex. Both are organised in a pyramid structure, mirroring each other all the way up with thousands of local divisions at the bottom, then various tiers of regional and provincial groups leading up to the national level at the apex. At the bottom, party and official government are clearly separated, and local-government officials are rarely Party officials. As you go up the tiers, however, Party and government intermingle more and more until at the top they are fused completely together, with all the key government positions occupied by leading Party members. That's why Hu Jintao is both general secretary of the Chinese Communist Party and president of the People's Republic.

At the apex of both Party and official government are National Congresses – the five-yearly National Party Congress for the Party and the yearly two-week long National People's Congress for the official government. Neither of these bodies, though, has any real power, and their role is essentially to rubber-stamp the choice of candidates for inner bodies for each. For the Party Congress, the inner body is the Central Committee; for the National People's Congress it is the Standing Committee. Each of these inner bodies has its own inner body. For the Party's Central Committee, this is the Politburo; for the People's Congress's Standing Committee, it's the State Council, which is China's nearest equivalent to a western government, being chaired by the premier and containing all the ministry heads. The 24-man Politburo and the 50-odd man State Council are the real power centres of China's government, but even these meet infrequently, and the hands-on control belongs to the inner circles, the nine standing members of the Politburo, headed by the General Secretary Hu Jintao and the 11-man Standing Committee of the State Council headed by Wen Jiabao.

The heart of power

In one way, the 3,000-strong National People's Congress is like China's parliament, and every bill must be passed through it before it becomes law. The State Council too is like

China's government, drafting the bills to put before the People's Congress and administering the country. But there is a good reason the People's Congress needs to meet for only two weeks every year. The behind-the-scenes negotiation means that pretty much every bill that comes before Congress has been agreed by the Party leadership already, and so is almost bound to go through. It is very rare indeed for a bill to be rejected, or for debate to be genuinely meaningful. There was heated debate at the 2006 Congress over the proposed law to protect private property (see pages 11–12), since this threw up such passionate differences between rightists who wanted to develop China's market economy even further and leftists who believed the property law was a step too far on the road towards capitalism. This kind of debate marked a new departure, though some pundits reckon it may become more common in future.

Politburo and State Council

So it is the Politburo Standing Committee and the State Council that are at the heart of Chinese power. Because leading Party members form the State Council, there is considerable overlap between the two. In the 1980s, Zhao Ziyang, a high-ranking government official, tried to make a clear separation of powers between them with the Politburo formulating policy and the State Council putting it into action, but they were so intertwined that it proved largely unworkable. That said, it is the Standing Committee of the Politburo that's China's power nexus, if anything is.

Beyond this, though, every political leader in the Party has his place in the pecking order. This is never formally published, but the protocol of rank is so firmly entrenched that the official state media always follow it – which means the stories are always ordered according to the ranking of the leader involved rather than the interest or importance of the story. When at official meetings and functions, too, leaders must always be seated according to their rank – or else there'll be trouble. In mid-2007, the ranking of the top six was: 1 Hu Jintao; 2 Jiang Zemin; 3 Wu Bangguo (chairman of the People's Congress Standing Committee); 4 Wen Jiabao; 5 Jia Qinglin; and 6 Zeng Qinghong (vice-president).

DIRTY CHINA

On 10 July 2007, one of China's leading officials, Zheng Xiaoyu, was executed for corruption. He was one of the highest ranking Chinese officials ever put to death, and his execution showed both how serious the Chinese leadership is about tackling corruption and how endemic the problem is. Mr Zheng was head of China's State Food and Drug Administration, and he rose to power as a reformer concerned to do something about China's safe drug supply. In the end temptation by bribes from players in the pharmaceutical business proved too much and gamekeeper turned poacher. In his confession, Zheng wrote, 'Why are the friends who gave me money all the bosses of pharmaceutical companies? Obviously because I was in charge of drug administration.'

Although Zheng was the highest profile culprit, corruption has been rife in Chinese politics for thousands of years. The CCP did manage to bring it under control in its early years, but the recent economic reforms have brought so many temptations that there has been a rising tide of dodgy practices in the last quarter century. In 1987 alone, 109,000 Party members were expelled for corruption, and since then hundreds have, like Mr Zheng, been executed for embezzlement each year. Every now and then the Party leadership launches campaigns against corrupt practices. In 1993, for instance, after Jiang Zemin became alarmed about excessive fondness of money, bribery, personal extravagance and illegal sex, the CCP Central Committee launched a clean-up drive. But this had limited effect, and in 1997, Jiang Zemin's renewed call for reform saw the setting up of the Spiritual Civilization Construction Guiding Committee. Yet the huge amounts of cash coming into China, and the huge worth of official contracts, has probably fuelled even more corruption since then. Mr Zheng was probably just the tip of a very, very large and mucky iceberg.

The People's Republic?

Outside China, there is considerable debate about the future of democracy in the country. Many commentators at one time felt certain that the opening up of China's economy to the rest of the world, and the growing influence of the market economy and private ownership, must lead to increasing pressure from Chinese people to have a say in their own government. If anything, though, China's growing prosperity has given the public faith in the wisdom of their government and has reduced the impetus for democracy within the country. Western observers are beginning to question if their optimism may have been misplaced. In an article in *Foreign Affairs* in July/August 2007, Azar Gat suggests that China, along with Russia, 'may represent a viable alternative path to modernity, which in turn suggests that there is nothing inevitable about the liberal democracy's ultimate victory – or future dominance'.

At the moment, China has very little democracy indeed. Since 1988, China's 930,000 villages have been allowed to elect local leaders, and since the mid-1990s, they have even been allowed to take part in the nomination of local Communist Party officials. But these are tokens, since the Party keeps a tight rein on who can be candidates, and popular preference never gets beyond the very lowest tiers. Some commentators say these moves may even delay real democracy by reducing demand for it.

TIANANMEN SQUARE

The lone student standing in front of a tank in Beijing's Tiananmen Square in June 1989 is firmly etched in the consciousness of the western world as one of the defining images of the twentieth century, and the massacre of hundreds of student protestors in the square by the Chinese army remains an ineradicable blot on the history of the People's Republic.

The reasons behind the protest are still being unravelled by historians, and the western version of what happened is still challenged by China's leaders. References to Tiananmen are one of the blocks put on Internet searches by the Chinese authorities, and publicly, the leaders will not depart from the official line that 'turmoil' had been 'justifiably quelled in order to maintain social stablity'.

In 1989, the economic reforms were just beginning to get under way. They had brought prosperity to some, but to others they had brought hardship as state enterprises began to close down. The leadership was locked in a bitter struggle over which way to go. On the one side were the Party elders, including Deng Xiaoping and Chen Yun, who believed the open economic door should by no means be an open political door. On the other was the Politburo headed by Zhao Ziyang who believed the Party should move towards 'the needs of building a socialist democracy'. With the two sides locked in combat, Beijing academics and students began to argue about the need for democracy and greater freedom. They worried that the Party elders would gain the upper hand and repression would return.

The death in April 1989 of Party leader Hu Yaobang, who democracy advocates felt had been on their side, prompted 500 students to demonstrate in Tiananmen Square. Five days later, half a million packed the square for Hu's funeral ceremony. Beijing students went on strike, but the square largely emptied, until a week later a provocative editorial in the People's Daily, inspired by

Deng, accused the students of launching a conspiracy and 'turmoil' to bring down the Party leadership. Immediately, half a million protesters flooded into the square, and many began to stay, some beginning a hunger strike. Zhao Ziyang, who had been in North Korea, came back and apologised for the editorial, and later even visited the students in the square.

As the square began to fill up, and the authorities seemed to be holding back, there was even a sense of optimism as students erected tents and began to play music, and some even felt that China might have its own velvet revolution. But the official plans for Mikhail Gorbachev's visit to Beijing from the 15 to 22 May were overshadowed by the protests, and the Chinese leadership felt humiliated. An intervention by Deng and the Party elders pushed Zhao out and proclaimed martial law. The army moved into the suburbs, but no further, and for two weeks, the protesters came to believe they would not do so. By this time, the students had been joined by Beijing workers, worried about the loss of jobs, and calling for proper participation in management in the workplace. Then on the terrible night of 3–4 June, the army moved in with tanks. No-one knows how many casualties there were, but there many hundreds – maybe up to a thousand. Despite the image of the student and the tank, it was ordinary Beijingers, who sought to prevent the army entering the square, who suffered the most casualties. After the massacre, there was a massive clampdown on anyone suspected of being a 'ringleader' with hundreds sent to labour camps, and many, it is believed, executed. It seemed a disastrous moment for China, and it justifiably blackened the country's image around the world. The people of Beijing in particular were shocked and saddened. And yet, remarkably, just three years later, Deng was able to appear on his Southern Tour, a smiling and benign old man, full of Confucius-like aphorisms, to champion the progress of reform. Zhao Ziyang, however, remained under house arrest, as he was for the rest of his life.

Protests and petitions

There's no doubt that China's people are not as docile as they once seemed to be – or rather, they have become braver at making their feelings show. Over the last ten to fifteen years, social protests such as riots, demonstrations, sit-ins and petitions have swollen in number, fuelled mostly by the growing wealth gap between the urban rich and the rural poor. Official statistics say there were as many as 85,000 such protests in 2005, compared with just 10,000 in 1994. Yet the protests are about local injustices, not a call for democracy. Protestors are up in arms about issues such as toxic spills from industry, the effect of dam projects and, above all, land grabs that take away farmers' land for development. Very rarely do they talk about the political system. Indeed, most protestors seem to believe that their grievances are caused by local officials and that if they can only get the chance to be heard by the leaders in Beijing, their wrongs will be addressed. There is some truth in this. Because China is such a huge country and the local officials are operating so far away – and keen to suppress news about protests – Beijing often does only get to hear about grievances when protestors make it to the capital.

Interestingly, Chinese citizens seem to be making their grievances known in ways surprisingly reminiscent of imperial days, when peasants would go to the emperor with a petition for justice. Between 1994 and 2004, the number of petitions to Beijing soared, reaching a staggering 13.7 million in 2004 alone. The government decided to reduce this tide of signatures by passing regulations to control it, and the number dropped by a million in 2005. They didn't, however, increase the number of petitions to which they responded. Chinese scholars hired by the government to study the matter believed that less than 0.2 per cent of the petitioners ever got an answer.

FALUN GONG

In the 1990s, as the power of the socialist ethic began to wane under the influence of market forces, some people, especially among the older generation, turned to religion and mysticism for reassurance. A plethora of Christian, Buddhist and Daoist sects began to multiply in the rural areas despite pressure from the atheist authorities, while in the cities many people began to explore ancient Chinese ideas in Qigong (the art of *qi*, the body's vital energy).

Qigong was part mystical and part martial art, and even some Chinese army leaders were taken up by 'Qigong fever'. One general apparently hoped that the qigong master Zhang Baosheng might be able to 'steal some nuclear secrets from the Russians or Americans'. Most of this went on with the approval of the authorities and received state funding via the Qigong association. But then a new sect called Falun Gong was established in north-east China by Li Hongzhi, a clerk and ex-army trumpeter who claimed to have been taught by a Buddhist master from an early age.

According to the group's literature, Falun Gong dates back to prehistoric times, but was only brought into the public eye when Li set up a study centre in Beijing in 1992. It combines Buddhist and Daoist beliefs with qigong exercises. Falun Gong means the Law of the Wheel, and the exercises are designed to help a person develop his or her wheel, the centre in the lower abdomen that is said to absorb energy from the universe.

At first it seemed like just an exercise regime, and hundreds of people, mostly old, would gather in squares to exercise. But Master Li withdrew Falun Gong from the Qigong association, maybe in a dispute about finance. This made Falun Gong illegal, and the authorities banned its publications. Falun Gong's response was surprisingly militant. In April 1999, thousands of Falun Gong members silently picketed the Communist Party headquarters in Beijing. After three months' deliberation, the movement was banned as an 'evil cult' and the authorities began to clamp down hard on members all over China, sending those who refused to recant their ideas to labour camps. From his safe refuge in New York, Li urged his followers to resist and a protest in Tiananmen Square led to hundreds of middle-aged protesters being dragged along the ground and bundled into police vans, provoking outrage from abroad.

The issue of Falun Gong continues to cause upset, not just in China but around the world. In February 2006, for instance, there was a row over the exclusion of Falun Gong from San Francisco's Chinese New Year Parade, which Falun Gong claimed was politically motivated.

Issue groups

As with petitions, so the number of issue groups has swelled dramatically in the last few decades. In 1988, there were just 4,500 non-governmental organisations (NGOs) in China. By 2005, there were 317,000. This is a huge number considering all of them have to register with the government and be sponsored by government organisations. Moreover, on top of the registered NGOs, the official news agency Xinhua estimates that there are more than 2.6 million unregistered groups. Most of these NGOs, even when formed to protest about something, are focused mainly on local environmental or social issues. Very rarely are they political. It seems likely that those that are have to operate far below the radar. According to an article by Carin Zissis in the *New York Times* (18 June 2007),

'In the past two years, authorities have stepped up investigations of foreign and domestic groups operating in China. Furthermore, authorities have pressurized activists to stop working for a particular NGO or risk endangering its funding or registration.'

The Chinese leadership is undoubtedly aware of the issue of democracy, and it has come up of course particularly in relation to Hong Kong. But they seem in no hurry to move in that direction at all, and as foreign investors find themselves more and more able to do very lucrative business with the Communist government outside pressure is, if anything, diminishing rather than increasing. In an article in February 2007, Wen Jiabao (Premier of China's State Council), wrote that the leadership was thinking about the first socialist stage of China's path to communism lasting a century, which implied that democracy would be very slow in coming to China.

THE GREAT FIREWALL OF CHINA

There is no doubt that the dramatic spread of Internet use in China has hugely expanded ordinary Chinese people's access to information. The Chinese authorities are concerned, of course, that if they allow unrestricted Internet access, they would find out just a little too much. So they have gone to huge trouble to make sure that people should only see what is 'healthy' and 'in the public interest'. Dissident opinions are not in the public interest and pornography is unhealthy. A 30,000 strong tech army now sit at computers policing website and emails filtering out anything which doesn't fit the bill in a system that has been dubbed the Great Firewall of China.

Some of it works by blocking out traffic from foreign websites entering China through its five electronic gateways. Some of it works by blocking keywords to prevent people searching for or entering offending sites. The country's 110,000 or so Internet cafés are also carefully vetted and continuously monitored by surveillance systems. The authorities also rely on self-censorship, and because of the fear of the punishments that can be meeted out against dissidents, this can be surprisingly effective. According to Amnesty International in 2006, 'Amnesty International is aware of at least 64 cyber dissidents who are imprisoned right now just for peacefully expressing their opinions online.' Foreign businesses are equally susceptible to self-censorship because of the threat of lost business. The American search engine Google was accused of selling out when it launched its Chinese version in 2005, since it was modified to exclude searches for such topics as Tiananmen Square and Falun Gong. Microsoft and Yahoo followed suit. Despite all this, Chinese people do have access to a wide range of content and some manage to find a way past the censors through blogs and by texting, but even blogs are coming under scrutiny.

Where next?

Although there is considerable speculation about China's policy direction for the next five years, and who will rise to the top, the truth is that no one knows outside the inner circle of the Chinese leadership – not even the country's Party members. No one even knows exactly when changes are going to happen. Most observers, though, believe Hu Jintao will lead the country even further in the direction in which he has been leading it over the past few years.

Mr Hu has shown that he is deeply aware of the divide that has opened up between rich and poor because of the country's economic boom, and aware too that those at the bottom have suffered from the removal of state support for health, housing, education and employment. So he is likely to introduce measures to deal with these problems, rather than reverse China's move towards an open market as his critics would like. Two weeks before the letter referred to at the beginning of this chapter, Hu made a speech emphasising that his two key goals were creating 'social harmony' and building a 'well-off society'. Coming from the mouth of a western politician, this would sound trite and meaningless, but in China it is a coded message with a very specific meaning, which every Communist Party member would understand. It means very specifically that the drive towards the market economy would continue in order to generate wealth, but also that the Party would take measures to take care of the less well-off to ensure that China is not disturbed by the problems and protests of the disadvantaged. Democratic rights were not mentioned.

GUANXI

Every month, hundreds of poor people from all over China turn up in Beijing at the government's petition office and queue patiently for days in order to register their own particular complaint. Most of them are victims of some sad injustice. A son has been beaten up or some land of theirs has been grabbed by a developer. They are convinced that if only the central government gets to hear of their case, their wrongs will be redressed. Sadly, most are mistaken. For nearly all of these petitioners, the quest is forlorn because they do not have the right *guanxi*; they just don't know the right people to pull the levers of power.

Guanxi is an untranslatable Chinese word, which is a combination of *guan* which means 'close' and *xi* which means 'be'. It can perhaps best be described as 'special relationship'. *Guanxi* is an ancient concept rooted in Confucian ideals of developing bonds of mutual obligation and trust and has come to play a central role in Chinese life, especially in politics and business. In order to get on in life, Chinese people develop a web of personal relationships beyond the family that can help them. You could call it networking, but it is actually far more personal and deep-rooted than that. It's not simply a question of chatting the right people up; 'pulling' *guanxi* is more about developing strong, dependable personal bonds. It is about developing ties that you do not break, through hard times as well as good. Politicians will reward those who stick with them through tricky times, because they have proven the strength of their *guanxi*. Businesses that stay with those in power when the going gets rough also prove the mettle of their *guanxi*. People doing business in China are often irritated by just how pervasive the power of *guanxi* is, and complain that it smacks of nepotism and cronyism – or worse still, inefficiency, as contracts are awarded on the basis of personal ties rather than competitive tendering. But the Chinese view it more as the kind of mutual support network that keeps society well-ordered and stable and gives talent a helping hand. Chinese business people place much more importance on developing trust and a personal bond with their clients than westerners. Visiting clients' homes, taking gifts and offering help might seem almost intrusive in the West, but in China, it is part of pulling *guanxi*. Only when your web of *guanxi* is well-developed, can you begin to 'walk' it.

CHAPTER 3   CITY AND FIELD

*'We saw unimaginable suffering and unthinkable helplessness,
unimagined resistance with incomprehensible silence, and have
been moved beyond imagination by unbelievable tragedy.'*
Chen Guidi and Wu Chuntao,
China's Peasants: an Investigation

In July 2007, Worldwatch reported the tragedy that befell a young construction worker in Guangdong. In a clash between migrant workers and company thugs, 27-year-old Lei Mingzhong was beaten over the head with a shovel, causing him fatal brain damage. Just what happened in poor Mr Lei's case is uncertain, but migrant workers like him are often the victims in China's rapidly changing society. There are some two hundred million of these workers, many desperately poor country people who have left their families behind to go and find work in the boom cities. They are forming a new underclass in China.

China's extraordinary economic growth has fuelled the most rapid urban growth the world has ever seen. Every week sees another half million added to China's city population. Every year sees China's cities grow by the equivalent of the population of Tokyo. Just a quarter of a century ago, four out of five Chinese people lived in the countryside, a higher proportion than most countries in the world. By 2000, the proportion living in cities had doubled. In a few years, more than half China's population, now 1.3 billion, will be city-dwellers. By 2020, just one in three Chinese people will be living in the countryside; while not far short of a billion people will be living in China's cities. China already has 60 cities with more than a million inhabitants. Over the next decade it will probably gain a handful of megacities with populations of thirty million or more – Beijing, Shanghai, Guangzhou and Chongqing – and a dozen cities the size of London (currently 7.5 million), such as Shenzhen and Tianjin.

Migrants on the move

With China's birth-rate in the cities limited by the one-child policy, it is clear that most of this expansion is not home grown in the cities, but comes from an enormous influx of people from the countryside. What's driving this migration, the biggest migration in human history by far, is both the pull of the cities with their promise of jobs and a better lifestyle, and the push of the countryside in which poverty can in places be as bad as anywhere in the world, despite half a century of Communist rule.

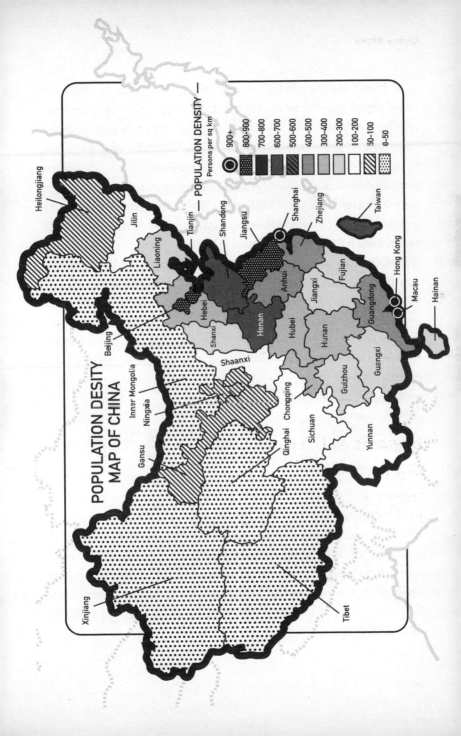

One of the problems for migrants is that their status in the cities is only temporary. In the early days of the Communist state, the details of every member of each family were recorded in a booklet called a *hukou*, lodged with the local police. This household registration not only dictated where you could work, but also where you could claim any welfare benefits. The *hukou* system made it very difficult for anyone to move from their home town or village, but it was especially restrictive for country people. City dwellers might occasionally move around or even between cities, but it was very rare for country people to stray more than a few miles from home.

The beginnings of the economic boom in the 1980s, however, created a huge demand for workers in the cities, which simply could not be met locally. So the government relaxed the

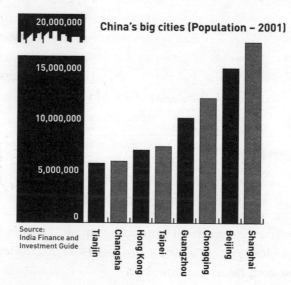

China's big cities (Population – 2001)

Source:
India Finance and
Investment Guide

restrictions to allow people to move around the country and apply for temporary residence permits, which they had to renew each month with the police. It was only meant to be a short-term, makeshift solution, but soon a tidal wave of migrants was sweeping in from the country, looking for work and a way out of the rural poverty trap. By 2000, there were some hundred and thirty million of these migrants. Now there are nearer two hundred million. Most of the migrants headed south to Guangdong or east to Shanghai and Beijing. In the south, 85 per cent of the city of Shenzhen's ten million inhabitants are migrants. Shanghai has well over four million migrants.

Without the labour of these migrants, who are generally prepared to work long hours for rock-bottom wages, China's economic boom would not have been possible, and the money they send back to their families in the country has alleviated the worst poverty of hundreds of millions of rural people. Almost 70 per cent of workers in manufacturing and construction and 32 per cent in the service industries are migrants. But this massive movement of people has caused a painful disruption to the social fabric of rural life.

ONE CHILD ONLY

Back in 1980, the Chinese government introduced one of the most controversial family planning laws ever dreamed up. Determined to slow down the growth of China's population which, they felt, was hampering China's prosperity, they limited all Chinese couples to just one child.

There were exceptions to the rule, such as ethnic minorities, and since 1980 a number of other 'exemptions' have been introduced, but otherwise the policy has been applied almost universally, especially in cities. A detailed scientific study by US and Chinese researchers reported in April 2007 that the policy, despite rumours to the contrary, has been extraordinarily effective. The lead author of the study, Wang Feng of the University of California, Irvine, said, 'Despite what some say, the policy has not been "relaxed" over the years... The system of exemptions resembles the American tax code in its complexity. But this does not change the fact that the one-child policy applies without exception to a significant majority [over two-thirds] of Chinese people.'

The result is that the average family size in China is under 1.5 people, and the Chinese population, at 1.3 billion, is a quarter of a billion less than it would have been otherwise. But although many would argue that this population restriction has helped alleviate much of the poverty and famine that once stalked China, the one-child policy has not been without painful or worrying consequences, even beyond the concern that it is an infringement of basic human rights.

First of all, the efforts to enforce the policy have led to all kinds of abuses by zealous officials. Countless women have been forced to have abortions, often at very late stages in their pregnancy – in some cases over eight months. Others have even had their wombs forcibly injected with saline solutions to ensure the child is stillborn. Many women, too, have been forcibly sterilised after the birth of a first child. For those couples who do succeed in having a second child, the penalties can be harsh. Fines are steep, and if the couple cannot afford to pay them, they may find their home stripped bare or even demolished by local officials. In May 2007, villagers in Guangxi were so distressed by attempts by local officials to increase the severity of punishments that they attacked government offices. According to a Reuters news report, one villager said, 'The family-planning officials were just like the Japanese invaders during the war. They took everything away, and destroyed or tore down the houses if people could not pay the fines.' Wealthier Chinese families, of course, can afford the fine, so simply pay up and have bigger families, fuelling resentment.

In the cities, the one-child policy is fairly universal, except for the rich, but in the country, people have found some ways round it. Families may send children off to relatives to avoid detection, or claim that siblings are actually adopted, or being looked after for a friend. Increasingly, in recent years, women have been turning to fertility drugs to increase the chances of multiple births. By having twins, triplets or even quads, mothers can have big families without falling foul of the one-child laws. With fertility drugs like Clomifene Citrate available cheaply over the counter, no questions asked, it is not surprising that some Chinese villages have seen an astonishing proliferation of twins and triplets.

All the same, despite these exceptions, the one-child

policy has been widely enforced, and it has had at least one sad and unforeseen consequence. Because of the traditional Chinese preference for sons, baby girls have been the key victims. As a result of the abortion of female foetuses, female infanticide and simple neglect of little girls, the ratio of boys to girls in China has gone up dramatically. The result is that there are over a million more boys born in China each year than girls. In 2007, 117 boys were born to every 100 girls. The imbalance is making it almost impossible for many Chinese men to find wives and girlfriends, and newspapers and internet sites are full of desperate Chinese men hoping to find a girl. Some become so desperate that there has been a tremendous rise in the exploitation and abuse of girls, with a low estimate of 42,000 girls kidnapped to be made slave wives or prostitutes every year. The Chinese government is so worried about the consequences of the male-female imbalance that they have issued instructions that anyone testing the gender of foetus without official permission would face 'serious punishment'. They also stated that they would increase their efforts to protect baby girls.

Another imbalance that the one-child policy is throwing up is the diminishing proportion of China's population that is young. Many experts predict that soon China will have a higher proportion of old people than most Western countries, with little of the wealth to support them. Nonetheless, the government remains as firmly wedded to the one-child policy as ever and aims to restrict China's population to between 1.6 and 1.7 billion in 2050.

Divided families

One of the reasons for this pain and disruption is just how difficult it is for migrants to go and work in the city. The temporary residence status of migrants means it is very hard for them to bring family members. Most have to go off to the city by themselves, leaving family and friends behind. The low

Number of people (millions) by age group

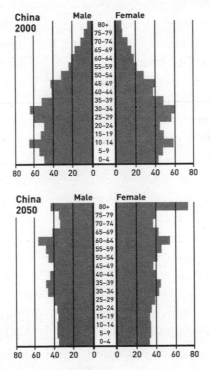

Source: US Census Bureau

83

SEXUAL SUPPRESSION

In 2006, a report in *China Daily* highlighted the sexual frustration of many migrant workers. A survey by the Health Ministry reported that 88 per cent of male migrants suffered from 'sexual depression' – and it's hardly surprising.

The work is so hard and conditions so poor, no migrant ever has a chance of finding a girlfriend, and husbands see their wives only a few times a year, if that. A survey carried out by the *Beijng Daily Star* showed that almost a quarter of married male migrants hadn't had sex in years, while almost half hadn't had sex with their wives for at least six months. Although there is no shortage of prostitutes for those who seek this way out, the wages of most migrants are so low that they cannot afford them.

Even when migrant couples are lucky enough to be working in the same city or even for the same company, their sex life is difficult to say the least. Many enterprises insist their employees live on site, but only provide single-sex dormitories. The *China Daily* trumpets a new initiative in Shenzhen in which the enterprise funded dozens of cheap apartments called 'lovebird nests', which can be rented when wives or husbands come to visit. But other solutions to the problem put forward by Chinese sociologists suggest that migrants are going to remain frustrated for some time to come. Their ideas include showing the workers 'healthy' movies and providing them with ping-pong and card tables – and, presumably, taking the odd cold shower or two.

wages and long hours mean that visits home are few and far between. Often, migrants only make it home once a year, at the Chinese New Year, when the trains and buses are packed solid with migrants clutching their red, white and blue bags (the reinforced plastic bags westerners use as laundry bags).

It is particularly hard for migrants who are married or have children. It is bad enough for the tens of millions of couples who are lucky if they see each other for just a few days each year. Even when both husband and wife turn migrant, they frequently have to head for different cities. But the real tragedy is for the children of migrants. The household registration system means children are only entitled to schooling in the place where they and their parents are permanently registered. So countless tearful fathers have to wave their children behind, knowing they will not see them for another year at least. Quite often, financial hardship means both parents have to leave their children in the hands of grandparents or relatives. It is estimated that 85 per cent of migrants with children in cities have had to leave their children behind in the countryside, and in many country regions over half the children have at least one, and often both, parents away working in the cities. To add to the sadness, China's one-child policy means many of these abandoned children have no siblings to keep them company.

Migrant schools

For every migrant with children there is a terrible decision to be made when they leave for the city. Either they can leave their children behind to ensure they get good schooling, or they can bring them along and subject them to a hard life in the city, with the knowledge that they may be completely deprived of education. Although many migrants' children are left behind, there are still vast numbers of them in each city. In 2003, Shanghai had three hundred thousand migrant children of school age; Shenzhen had four hundred thousand.

When the migrants first began to arrive in the cities, they could sometimes get their child a place at a city school, but only by paying a fee that was way beyond most of them. Desperate for a solution, some migrants banded together to set up their own schools. These migrant schools were illegal, and frequently shut down by the authorities – and even when they did stay open they had to rely for funding entirely on the small fees they charged to migrants. Some migrants couldn't even afford these fees, and UNICEF estimated that, in 2003, 10 per cent of migrant children got no schooling at all The authorities tried to solve the problem by leaning on city schools to take in some of the migrant children, but as class-sizes crept up to 45 or more, the intake slowed down.

Chinese sociologists are beginning to worry about a whole generation of tens of millions of children, who have been brought up either deprived of parental love or guidance in the countryside, or deprived of proper schooling in the city. There are real concerns about a society in the future polarised between the adult manifestations of these 'lost children' of migrants on the one hand, and the 'little emperors' of wealthier city folk (see pages 206–208) on the other.

NO MIGRANTS HERE, PLEASE

Beside their difficult personal lives, many migrants have to cope with discrimination that may in some ways be even more extreme than that suffered by migrant arrivals in western cities in the twentieth century. The migrants may be Chinese, like the cities' permanent residents, but they are usually instantly recognisable by their manner and their 'rustic-style clothes' – and they have only temporary resident status.

One of the problems is that they have no legal status, which means they can be mercilessly exploited by employers. Most migrant workers earn not just below average wages, but often well below the national minimum – and work incredibly long hours in poor and often unsafe conditions. To make matters worse, their wages are often left unpaid for months at a time, and because they have no contract, they have no way of forcing the issue. The case of Mr Li quoted at the beginning of this chapter is typical. Mr Li was one of a group of migrant workers who went on strike after going for over four months without any pay – only to be met by a gang of thugs hired by their employer. But after hundreds of abducted children and adults were found working virtually as slaves in brick kilns and mines in Shanxi and Henan in July 2007, the government was spurred into action and passed a law that requires employers to provide written contracts from 2008.

Whether it makes any difference remains to be seen – but another bit of legislation enacted recently did make a difference. A few years ago, migrants were picked on by police who were entitled to check their residence documents and deport them from the city. But in 2003 the death in police custody of migrant designer Sun Zhigang in Guangzhou created such a stir that the government changed the law, so that migrants did not have to carry their residence documents. This has, apparently, made a huge difference to migrants.

Changing cities

The cities that all these migrants are arriving in have changed dramatically from the way they were just twenty years ago. They have not just got much bigger; they have changed dramatically in character too. Twenty years ago, most of them were quite sleepy places that had barely changed since the time of the emperors. Cities such as Suzhou on the Grand Canal north of Shanghai had changed very little since the time of Marco Polo (in the thirteenth century), when it was described as the Venice of the east for its ancient canalside gardens and teahouses. In Beijing, though it had its modern quarters, most people still lived much they had done for hundreds of years in the districts where old single-storey courtyard houses are packed together along narrow alleyways called *hutongs*. Traffic could not penetrate into the *hutongs*, and in the shelter between the houses, or in the courtyards inside, life was very simple and communal, with people coming and going, gossiping, cooking, bathing, playing chess or simply watching the world go by.

The traditional Chinese city is fast disappearing as China goes on a building frenzy larger than the world has ever seen, consuming half the world's cement and occupying more than half its cranes. The results are most spectacular in Beijing and Shanghai, where scores of skyscrapers, apartment blocks and new buildings are going up each year, to create city centres that make New York's Manhattan look old-fashioned, but it is going on in cities across China, from Wenzhou to Shenzhen, from Xiamen to Chongqing. City officials are desperate to see their city is not left behind and are pushing development on at an ever faster pace.

Demolition mania

With space at a premium in some places, old houses are simply bulldozed out of the way to make room for the construction work. Giant new highways are carved through ancient housing districts in much the way railways sliced through Victorian cities. Concrete and glass towers soar in weeks from the dust of demolished *hutongs*. Such is the sense of urgency that the demolition work goes ahead even before it has been decided what to put in its place, with many cities left with rubble-strewn gaps, stranded like gap teeth amid the building sites. City planning officials seem to be constantly rushing round with paint brushes to daub the character *chai* on old buildings, inspiring some Chinese people to joke grimly that at last the country is living up to its foreign name, China, which sounds all too much like *chai-ne* or 'demolish it' in Mandarin. In his book *Getting Rich First* (2007), Duncan

Hewitt tells of another black joke doing the rounds in Shanghai where the pace of change is especially rapid. Apparently, you should always remember to ring in advance the restaurant where you're planning to eat – not to book a table but to check it hasn't been knocked down.

Many Chinese people are glad to see the back of the old houses. They are difficult to modernise, facilities are basic and the lanes are often too narrow for cars and delivery vehicles to gain access. People used to living in drafty, smelly conditions with only basic sanitation are often pleased as punch to move to modern apartments with views over the city. But often people have been booted out of their old houses even when they didn't want to go – and sometimes in a fairly ruthless manner, with insufficient compensation. There are stories of old people who refused to move being beaten up by gangs of heavies. Moreover, those evicted from the old houses are not always rehoused.

Even where the demolition has gone ahead smoothly and amicably there are those who are devastated to see so much of China's heritage being swept away with a zealousness that is reminiscent of the Cultural Revolution. Some people say that preserving the *hutong* is a romantic luxury for foreigners and intellectuals. 'You only need to watch an elderly grandmother walking across thick ice at 5 a.m. to go to the public toilet to be dispelled of [the idea of preserving Beijing's *hutongs*],' says Jha Aimei in an article quoted in the *Christian Science Monitor*. However, more and more people are beginning to wake up to the destruction. The message is beginning to sink in at the highest level, too. In June 2007, a young woman called Xia

Jie conducted a brave last-ditch campaign to save her home *hutong* in Beijng, the Dongsi Batiao where many of the houses date back to the thirteenth century. Remarkably, Xia Jie's campaign succeeded in getting the demolition suspended. The suspension may turn out to be short-lived, but China's vice minister of construction talked to the press about the 'senseless actions' of bureaucrats that have devastated China's national sites and relics, saying 'Some local officials seem to be unaware of the value of cultural heritage.' He is right. It is not just beautiful old houses. Ming dynasty temples and ancient archaeological sites have all come under the demolition men's hammers. One team even knocked down a section of the Great Wall to create a road for construction lorries...

New lifestyle

The sufferings of the migrant workers and the destruction of China's old buildings is the downside of China's economic boom. But there are, for many Chinese people, far more pluses than minuses. However difficult the migrant workers' lives are, the wages they earn and send back to their families has done more than anything to improve people's lives in the countryside. Many country people who were living in shacks are now able to afford solid houses, and acquire basic consumer goods such as TVs, refrigerators, mobile phones and even motor bikes – all things that would have been far beyond them not so long ago. And the migrant workers themselves are making progress. Many are putting down roots in their adopted city, and beginning to adapt to permanent city life, and put aside enough money to find reasonable accommodation, even though these workers are still the minority.

It is the permanent city residents, though, who have witnessed the most dramatic changes in their lifestyles, and benefited from them the most. City wages are on average three times what they are in the countryside, and although the cost of living in cities is much higher, the lucky ones have begun to acquire a lifestyle that was completely unimaginable to Chinese people just a quarter of a century ago.

For the visitor, the most obvious signs of the new China are the flashy new buildings, the fast-food restaurants, the shopping malls with shops selling all the major labels, from Nike to Armani, and all the latest high-tech items, from iPhones to plasma TVs. But the most profound changes, perhaps, are behind closed doors.

Independent living

Until the 1990s, most housing was controlled by the state, with most city dwellers living in homes allocated by their work unit. Houses were often shared, not just between the extended family, but between many families. Yet although they were far from ideal, they were very cheap and the state made sure everyone was housed. But in 1998, along with the other changes, the Chinese leadership took the huge step of doing away with low-cost social housing. Rents in existing homes rose significantly, and all new houses can now only be bought, not rented. In some ways, it was a bit like Margaret Thatcher's sell-off of council houses in the UK in the 1980s, but even more drastic – and it is perhaps no coincidence that the architect of the scheme had paid a visit to Mrs Thatcher, whom he was said to admire.

With the cushion of social housing taken away, people suddenly realised they would have to provide their own homes in future, and within a few years, when the implications sank in, owning a home became the top priority for most Chinese city dwellers. Even when renting was much simpler and easier, people were determined to buy to secure their future – perhaps not surprising for old people worried by the gradual reduction in pensions and young men who suddenly found themselves unmarriageable unless they had a home. Not surprisingly, there has been a property boom in Chinese cities, but the scale of this boom has been breathtaking for a country that just a decade or so earlier had been an essentially poor communist country. Between 1998 and 2005, the value of home mortgages taken out by Chinese people rose 35-fold to about £130 billion.

Retail expression

On the one side, this urge to purchase has put tremendous pressure on some people, who have become mortgage slaves, or have simply been priced out of the city areas that were once their homes. On the other, many young people have at last been able to move out from under their parents' roofs and find a home of their own. In the past, young couples, even when they were married, would have little or no privacy, living in a house shared with their extended family, often without a room of their own – and nowhere to go to be themselves, and enjoy the (very different) things contemporary youngsters enjoy. Now every urban couple aspires to own their own modern flat, in which they can, as they see it, express their own sense of style.

This style is frequently Ikea, which has had a bigger impact on Chinese tastes even than it did in Europe. These young Chinese urbanites are completely new to the idea of styling their homes. Going to the giant Ikea branches is like going to the most exciting home exhibition, where Ikea's style consultants are on hand to give guidance. Minimalist, with white walls and giant flat-screen TV, is currently the most popular style, but this will probably change just as quickly as it is changing in the western world. Many of the most arty, on-the-ball Shanghaiers are going 'bobo' – bourgeois bohemian, with Tibetan-style ethnic furniture and restored warehouse apartments and even *hutong* houses. A few are even beginning to buy antique Chinese furniture – literally thrown out by most just a few years ago in the rush to get a modern decor.

Getting around

Second on the list of major purchases after a house, of course, is a car, and car ownership in cities is going up by five million vehicles a year (and rising), making China one of the world's biggest markets for new cars. On the whole, these are status symbols, used for driving around the increasingly clogged city roads, rather than on long journeys. China's tens of thousands of miles of new motorways are used largely by commercial traffic. The bicycle, once the mainstay of Chinese personal transport, is falling by the wayside.

Land grab

One perhaps unforeseen effect of the breakneck expansion of cities has been the huge amount of prime farmland that has been concreted over. A total of nearly 7 million hectares has been lost to urban development in the last twenty years. Far from being restricted by regulations such as Green Belt plan-

---

EUROSTYLE

For the better off, the highpoint of chic is often a European- or American-style residence. New, top of the range housing developments in Beijing are being built in a curious hybrid of styles inspired by everything from chateaux to Italian villas. Developments even have European or American names, such as Regents Gardens or Versailles Island. The whole idea, of course, is that you acquire the kind of life that goes with the style of house you buy. Californian, Spanish, French and British are most popular, but New Yorker and Italian also have their fans. Around Shanghai, a series of satellite towns has been built, each in a remarkably accurate pastiche of a particular European country. The British town is called ThamesTown, and comes complete with Georgian squares, red telephone boxes and English-style pubs.

---

ning laws, Chinese urban expansion is encouraged by development goal setting and aided by regulations that give almost unlimited powers to local officials to take over land when they want. More and more stories come out each year about poor farmers pushed off their land with scant compensation to make way for development projects that line the pockets of local officials and developers alike, leaving the farmers with little or nothing, and robbing China of valuable land for food production. Many of the most violent disturbances now are occurring not in the cities but on the urban fringes where farmers have lost their livelihoods.

China's cities and regions	%GDP	Mob Phone ownership (millions)	Internet users (millions)	Life expectancy	Literacy (%)
Shanghai	5.5	13.1	4.4	78.1	91.8
Beijing	3.1	13.4	4.0	76.1	94.7
Hong Kong	N/A	N/A	2.5	81.6	N/A
Shandong	11.3	19.1	8.5	73.9	88.8
Jiangsou	11.3	22.3	6.6	73.9	85.7
Guangdong	11.7	53.7	11.9	73.9	93
Sichuan	4.8	115.1	5.2	71.2	86.5
Qinghai	0.3	1.2	0.2	66	75.2
Inner Mongolia	2.0	5.9	0.9	69.9	86.5
Xinjiang	1.6	4.9	1.2	67.9	91.8
Tibet	0.2	0.4	0.1	64.4	56.2

Source: China Statistical Yearbook, 2005

The rural lag

In some ways, China's farmers have been left behind by the economic boom that has transformed the country's cities. The irony that it was the peasant farmers who were meant to be the leading edge of Mao's revolution not so long ago is not lost on many Chinese people. One of the first and most drastic changes the Communists made when they came to power was to take away land from landowners and hand it to the peasants – an action that cost the lives of a million or more landlords. Gradually, though, Mao took the land back from the peasants and gathered both them and the land together in giant collective farm production units known as People's Communes in the late 1950s (see pages 247–8). The communes were such a disaster – first because of dreadful crop yields, and second because grain was sent to cities before the peasants were fed – that thirty million or more people died in the world's worst famine, between 1958 and 1961 – all the more shocking because it was entirely human-made.

THE SADNESS OF WOMEN

China is the only country in the world where women are more likely to commit suicide than men. One woman kills herself in China every four minutes, and another one tries to do so every twenty seconds or so. The problem is particularly bad in rural areas, where the suicide rate is three times higher than in towns. One reason, according to Chinese researcher Xu Rong, is simply the availability of pesticides in rural areas. But drinking pesticides is a clear sign of the hard life some country women have to live.

Many traditional attitudes towards women have survived the communist revolution and arranged marriages where the groom's parents buy the bride are still common. Once married, a young wife is taken from her home and immediately becomes the workhorse for all her in-laws. Education has made this traditional role harder for some girls to bear and they are frequently trapped into conflict with their husband with no prospect of escape.

The one-child policy has underlined how little-valued girls are as many female foetuses are aborted and some baby girls are murdered. It has also led to a shortage of women. For every hundred girls born in China, 117 boys are born and, by 2020, there will be 40 million more young men than women. Xie Lihua, editor of one of China's leading women's magazines, believes this will put girls in an even more vulnerable position, worrying that 'Abduction and trafficking will increase. So will prostitution, as well as sexual violence against women and rape.' Organisations in China are now trying to develop programmes to set up village support groups and confidence training courses.

'Chinese farmers show the way'

Finally, in the 1970s, the leadership acknowledged the failure of the communes and divided the land up amongst individual families again. The official story, well known to most Chinese people, is that eighteen farmers in Xiaogang in Anhui, desperate to find a better way to feed their families, decided secretly to split their collective farmland so that each had his own plot. They would together pay the grain tax due for the collective, but otherwise they would grow food for themselves, and sell any surplus. The arrangement was highly illegal, and could have resulted in execution, but it worked and, so the story goes, word got back to Deng Xiaoping, who in 1980 introduced the 'Household Responsibility System' under which families were allowed to farm their own plot with crops of their choice, and sell any surplus.

The effect was immediate. Agricultural production began to rise, and many farmers were soon not only feeding their families well but also earning money by selling produce in the 'free markets' that started up in many Chinese towns in the 1980s. Many farmers began to see marked improvements in their lives, and were able to buy things for the first time, stimulating a slight consumer boom in the countryside, raising rural living standards.

Some of the farmers began to look for ways to use that money to make more money and many pooled their savings to start up little factories allowed by Deng Xiaoping called 'township and village enterprises' (TVEs). TVEs began to mushroom in the 1980s, some started by groups of farmers, some as private investments by local governments. Most were tiny companies employing fewer than half a dozen people, and doing things like processing food or making spare parts for farm equipment, but some have flourished and developed into major industrial corporations – particularly in the south in Guangdong. There are now an astonishing 120 million TVEs, and they have played a key part in China's economic boom. Although most are just tiny enterprises making little more than pocket money, they have provided a rich training ground for China's peasants in becoming business people and entrepreneurs. Some are now selling produce all round the world.

Rural poor

Unfortunately, despite the success of the TVEs, the improvements in farm incomes were not sustained, for a variety of reasons. Most plots, for instance, are far too small for mechanisation and economies of scale. Many have been hit by water shortages as cities and agricultural production drain China's rivers dry. Others suffer from soil erosion as land is over used and widespread deforestation exposes fields to the wind. When China joined the World Trade Organization in 2001, Chinese farmers also faced cut-price competition from foreign producers working on large farms.

Average incomes have been improving in the countryside, but at half the rate they are in the cities, with rural incomes staying at a third of those in the cities, and the averages disguise a far bleaker picture that exists in some parts of the country, especially the west. One of the problems is that nearly all the development money that has been spent in China has gone into industry and the cities. Almost none has gone into agriculture.

To make matters worse, social support began to collapse in

rural areas, as the government dismantled the welfare system and concentrated what support they gave on the cities. In 1998, the government broke up the Ministry of Education with a disastrous effect on rural education. A World Bank survey showed that four out of ten children in some poor rural areas received no education whatsoever. Medical care was, if anything, even worse. In Mao's days, 'barefoot doctors' – people trained in basic medical skills – had gone out into every part of the country and brought good basic medical care to even the poorest. This system, though, was based around the collectives, and when the collectives disappeared in the 1980s, their medical care went with them. A few richer farming areas set up their own health schemes. Official figures in 2002 showed that only 7 per cent of China's eight hundred million peasants had basic medical cover, compared with 90 per cent in 1979. The Health Ministry acknowledged that in the early years of the twenty-first century two-thirds of country people who needed hospital treatment did not get it.

The worst thing, perhaps, was the power of greedy local officials over the lives of the peasants. In December 2003, husband and wife Chen Guidi and Wu Chuntao wrote a shocking report entitled *China's Peasants: an Investigation*, which caused such a massive stir when it was published that 200,000 copies sold very quickly, and, after a government ban, sold a further 7 million copies on the black market. Many more read it on the Internet. The book began life when Wu Chuntao learned of a peasant woman who bled to death after the birth of her child because she could not afford the US$360 demanded by her local hospital for treatment. Chen and Wu then spent three years travelling round Anhui and trying to find out the causes of the peasants' problems. The stories they told were enough to make many readers alternately weep with sadness or cry out with rage, as peasants were exploited and abused by corrupt local officials, and economically squeezed by the escalating taxes they had to pay, which more than wiped out any increase in farm incomes. It was hardly any surprise that so many peasants were just giving up and migrating to the cities, often leaving good agricultural land to go to weed.

Getting better

The Chinese government began to realise there was a problem, and bumped up the money put aside for agriculture by 15 per cent in 2006. This pushed China's annual farm development budget to US$42 billion. That sounds like a lot, but with eight hundred million people living in the countryside, the increase was worth just US$7 per person.

RURAL PROTESTS

All over China, the expansion of cities is causing conflict as development robs peasant farmers of their land. The government is now receiving tens of thousands of petitions from peasants convinced that if only central government gets to hear of the problems going on locally, the injustice against them will be righted.

In an article in the *New York Times* in December 2004, Jim Yardley tells the poignant story of the villagers of

Sanchawan in Shaanxi. When officials from the nearby city of Yulin seized a huge area of their farmland for development, they tried every form of protest they could think of. Men from the village went to Beijing, to try and get a hearing for their case, but could not break through the wall of bureaucracy. 'For thousands of years, the relationship between farmers and their land has been as thick as blood, as close fitting as lips and teeth,' they wrote in one of their petitions, but their appeal had no effect. After the Yulin city officials seized even more land, the desperate villagers staged a sit-in, refusing to farm – which was a provocative act since local officials have to meet production targets. Police were then sent in to break up the sit-in with such violence that the villagers were cowed into submission.

In his book *Getting Rich First*, Duncan Hewitt cites the equally poignant case of 25,000 villagers who were simply chucked out of their homes on the Taizi River in north-east China to make way for a reservoir. Some were eventually given land so poor it was almost useless for farming; others were given nothing at all and were reduced to beggary. For seven years, the villagers campaigned for justice, but only got attention when each of their nine representatives travelled to Beijing and threatened to cut off a little finger and lay it before the government offices. Eventually, their case was reviewed and, when they received compensation, it was hailed by the media as a breakthrough – but the compensation was a mere US$16 each.

However, it was a start, and the same year, the government decided to scrap the tax on agricultural products, which was the biggest burden to farmers, and then went on to scrap a whole host of other rural taxes. These were all part of a wider programme called 'Creating a New Socialist Countryside', designed to address rural problems such as poor education and healthcare. The tax cuts have already begun to have an effect in some areas, and there are small but definite signs of growing prosperity – so marked, that many rural workers were choosing to stay in the country to work on the land, and many migrants were even coming back from the cities at last. Official reports are showing that farm incomes are climbing, and there is considerable optimism that China's farms may well have turned a corner.

CHAPTER 4   DIRTY CHINA?

'If I work in your Beijing, I would shorten my life at least five years.'

**Chinese Prime Minister Zhu Rongji
to Beijing officials in 1999**

In January 2007, the Chinese official environmental watchdog the State Environmental Protection Administration (SEPA) reported that 2006 had been China's dirtiest year ever. Pan Yue, SEPA's vice-head, admitted that '2006 has been the most grim year for China's environmental situation'. And that was quite a feat. China's record on pollution and the environment is nothing short of disastrous. While hurtling along at breakneck speed on its path of economic development, it has created a huge mess of environmental problems.

Serious spills of industrial effluent into water occur every other day, with 161 incidents recorded (and many unrecorded) in 2006 alone. Levels of sulphur dioxide have doubled over the last decade to make China the most sulphur dioxide-polluted place on earth – creating acid rain that falls over a third of the country and has badly damaged forests as far afield as Japan. Sixteen of the world's twenty most polluted cities are in China, including Linfen, the worst of all, and the Chinese government report revealed that two-thirds of China's three hundred biggest cities had air quality well below the World Health Organization's minimum standards.

The catalogue of pollution woes goes on. A World Bank report concluded that seven hundred and fifty thousand people died prematurely in Chinese cities in 2006 because of air pollution. A further sixty thousand are believed to have died from poor-quality water, which causes severe diarrhoea, liver and bladder cancers. SEPA estimates that 70 per cent of the water in five out of China's seven major river systems is so polluted that it is unfit for human contact, let alone drinking. An estimated 90 per cent of urban water supplies are contaminated with organic and industrial waste. Barely half of China's sewage is treated before being discharged into rivers and the filthy water helps China suffer over eight hundred million cases of diarrhoea each year. And, to cap it all, in 2006 China overtook the USA much earlier than expected as the world's biggest emitter of the greenhouse gas carbon dioxide.

BAG END

When you are given a plastic carrier bag to take your shopping home from the supermarket, the chances are that bag was made in Shenzhen, by companies such as Delux Arts Plastics, which churns out three-quarters of a million new bags a month. Once they are used, the bags go back to almost the same place in China, to be 'recycled'. EU law forbids the dumping of waste abroad, but it allows it be shipped to China for recycling. There are plenty of centres for recycling in China for all kinds of products, but at the bottom of the chain are the bag and bottle recyclers of places such as Shunde and Heshan, where whole neighbourhoods are piled high with toxic piles of smelly old bags waiting to be chopped, melted and moulded into pellets by poorly paid workers. After a series of reports in British media damning the dreadful conditions in these recycling villages in February 2007, the Chinese government decided to shut down the worst offenders and ban the import of foreign waste. But some people depend on the business for their livelihood and have simply moved to different sites and found different ways to get the waste.

Land and water

Unfortunately, the environmental problems don't end with pollution. China has the some of the world's worst water shortages. Lack of water has always been a problem in a country where the water resources per capita are less than a quarter of the world average. China's Water Ministry says that four hundred of China's biggest cities are short of water. In the arid north, 80 per cent of the wetlands have dried up along the region's major river system, the Huang Ho, which is actually so drained of water that it is in danger of drying up before it reaches the sea. Further south, droughts are ruining crops even along the Yangtze, China's main river. In Chonqing and Sichuan two-thirds of rivers dried up altogether in 2006.

Fields and forests in China are fast disappearing, too, as they are being eroded from both sides by deserts and cities. In just the last decade, 6 million hectares of China's best arable land has been buried beneath concrete, while deserts are expanding all over the country as a result of over-exploitation of water resources and over-grazing.

Green issues

With all this, it is hardly surprising that green campaigners identify China as an environmental disaster zone, and urge China to put the brakes on the economic development, which they fear will make the situation worse. Many western economists also argue that the environmental crisis will make economic progress unsustainable anyway, as cities choke and its industries run out of clean water to increase production – or are deprived of workers who succumb to pollution-related illnesses. Meanwhile, the human cost is high, and perhaps it is not surprising that there has been a rising tide of public protest about environmental matters within China. In fact, environmental issues, such as toxic spillages and water shortages, stir ordinary Chinese people into active protest more than any other issue. In May 2007, thousands took to the streets of Xiamen in Fujiang and stopped the building of a petrochemical plant. In 2005, at least three people were killed by police in Dongzhou in Guangdong during riots over a planned power plant.

From this catalogue of woes, it would be very easy to get the idea that China is recklessly ploughing on towards environmental catastrophe, heedless of the consequences. This is far from the truth. There is a deep awareness at the very top level of government of the problems, and this has been the case for some years. Indeed it may be true to say the Chinese government has been more proactive in trying to deal with environmental problems than any other in the world. When Prime Minister Wen made his annual major speech in March 2007, he put environmental issues right at the top of the government's priorities. Wen admitted that China is failing on key energy and pollution goals, and that unless it became more energy-efficient and protected the environment better, the country's much cherished economic boom could suffer badly.

The challenge for Wen and the Chinese government is that the problems they have to deal with are gigantic, and they are wary of clamping down too hard and disrupting the economic growth that so many Chinese are relying on to lift them out of poverty. As Chinese environment official Lu Xuedu said at a conference in October 2006, 'You cannot tell people who are struggling to eat that they need to cut their emissions.'

The environmental problems they need to deal with fall into four areas: energy, water, land and pollution. The biggest is energy.

Dirty power

For a country with limited natural energy resources, China is astonishingly profligate. Inefficient factories and poor building construction mean huge amounts of energy are wasted every day. It's hard to be sure just how much energy is lost, but one very simple statistic paints the picture: for every dollar of its gross domestic product (GDP), China uses three times as much energy as the world average. For every dollar of its GDP, China uses eleven-and-a-half times as much energy as Japan.

What makes the situation worse is that because China has limited oil and gas resources, most of its energy comes from coal. Over 70 per cent of China's energy comes from coal, both for generating power and for heating houses, and China accounts for 90 per cent of the world increase in coal consumption over the last four years. Like burning oil, burning coal produces a lot of the greenhouse gas, carbon dioxide, but it also chucks a lot of soot into the air, and a large amount of acid-rain-causing sulphur dioxide – especially if it is poor quality and sulphurous, as much of China's coal is. China already produces almost twice as much sulphur dioxide as the USA, and the amount is rising rapidly.

As China's industry expands, its energy demands are likely to expand too. Already, China's raging thirst for oil is creating major disturbances in the world oil market (see pages 133–4), but importing more oil is unlikely to do much for the country's environmental problems. Most of that extra oil will go into the millions of new cars that are flooding onto China's new motorways every year. A few decades ago, China used to have some of the world's greenest transport with its million of bicycles. Those days are gone as increasing prosperity encourages Chinese people to join the rest of the world behind the wheel. So China's power generation is likely to rely on coal for the foreseeable future. To meet its energy needs, China is building the equivalent of two 600 megawatt coal-fired power stations every week. In 2006 alone, China added more generating capacity than the entire generating capacity for the state of California – and 90 per cent of this increase was in coal-fired stations.

Car use is currently still so low in China that it contributes almost nothing to the country's desperate air-pollution problems, but the number of cars is rising fast (see pages 94–95). Yet coal-fired power stations, domestic coal burning and uncontrolled factory emissions are quite enough to give most of China's cities air so filthy that these cities are invisible from satellites on many days of the year. Car ownership in China is tiny in proportion with that of the developed world, with only 1 in 60 Chinese people owing a car, compared with 1 in 2 Americans. Green campaigners worry that if car ownership in China ever reaches even a tenth of the level it is in the USA, the pollution could make some Chinese cities unlivable.

CHINA AND GLOBAL WARMING

For some people, the failure of China to agree to binding targets to reduce its soaring greenhouse gas emissions is one of the biggest problems facing the fight against global warming. One of George Bush's main arguments for pulling out of the Kyoto process (the Kyoto Protocol is an international agreement drawn up in 1997, which places mandatory greenhouse gas emission targets on industrialised countries that have signed up to the agreement) was that it placed no requirements on China to cut greenhouse gas emissions. Without China properly in the mix, he felt, the Kyoto protocol was meaningless. When China overtook the USA as the world's biggest carbon-dioxide emitter, it seemed only to back the American case up.

China's argument, however, was that it had contributed only a very tiny proportion of the greenhouse gases already in the atmosphere that are causing most of the warming effect. Moreover, because of China's large, poor population, cheap energy is essential for its development. 'If you only visit Beijing, Shanghai, Hong Kong, you see one China,' said Lu Xuedu (the deputy director-general of China's Office of Global Environmental Affairs) in evidence to the UK joint committee on climate change, 'But if you go the countryside or just two hours' drive from Tiananmen Square, you see a totally different situation.'

However, the Chinese government is aware that with major water shortages and droughts hitting the country already, they could be one of the earliest victims of climate change, so in June 2007, they introduced their own independent plan for cutting greenhouse gas emissions. The plan states right at the start that, 'The country will not impose carbon dioxide emission caps, which would hurt a developing nation trying to eradicate poverty', but it includes a number of measures to help mitigate climate change, such as phasing out the production of gas-guzzling cars and planting trees to boost the country's forest cover from 14 per cent in the 1990s to 20 per cent by 2010. Climate change campaigners point out that the urgency of the situation requires far more drastic action than this and, however unfair it is, China must join the rest of the world in slowing greenhouse gas emissions now. The slight shift in American attitudes shown under pressure from Tony Blair at the 2007 G8 summit in Heiligendamm in Germany may in time persuade China, too, to come aboard a more global approach.

Cleaning up

The ray of hope, though, is that the Chinese government seems to be more aware than many foreign critics give it credit for of the scale of the problems it is facing. First of all, it is trying to slow the rise in energy use. In its current five-year plan, which runs until 2010, it has committed to reducing the country's energy intensity – that is, the amount of energy consumed for every unit of GDP – by 20 per cent. Of course, since

China's GDP is increasing by near enough 10 per cent a year, all this means is that they are hoping to peg back the increase in energy consumption to just 8 per cent a year. So far, they are falling behind this target, as SEPA admits, but some progress has been made.

Second, it is trying to clean up its act on coal-fired power stations. Each year, now, it is spending some US$70 billion on introducing smokestack scrubbers and similar measures to clean up the emissions. It is also concentrating on building big power stations that are able to produce power more efficiently than the countless small ones China has relied on in the past.

Third, it is looking at alternative sources of fuel. Perhaps surprisingly, China is already the world's largest user of alternative energy, and it is looking to expand its use of wind-power generators. More than sixty huge wind farms have already been built in the west of the country and more are on their way. Hydro-electric power brings its own problems (see Three Gorges below). Unfortunately, renewables still account for barely 7 per cent of China's energy needs, and as energy consumption keeps rising, the expansion of alternative energy supplies is barely keeping pace.

THREE GORGES

In 2007, the gigantic walls of the Three Gorges dam project in Hubei province were completed. When the generators are installed and operating in 2009, it will complete by far the biggest hydro-electric project in the world. The 180-metres (600-feet) high dam across the Yangtze River has created a reservoir that when full will be over 640 kilometres (400 miles) long and more than a hundred metres deep.

The hope is that the dam will finally tame the notorious floods of the Yangtze that have claimed more than a million lives in the past century. It will also allow 10,000-tonne ocean-going freighters to sail right into China's interior for six months of the year. And its 26 giant turbines will generate up to a ninth of all China's power needs.

That the project is almost complete, and on schedule, is a phenomenal achievement, but critics say the cost has been, and will be, too high. Already, over a million people have been moved from their homes to make way for the project, and twelve hundred villages and two large towns will be swamped beneath the rising waters behind the dam. Green campaigners say the water behind the dam is already heavily polluted by the effluent from drowned factories, while restricting the flow of the Yangtze will worsen pollution downstream. Historians claim that thirteen hundred key archaeological sites will drown beneath the reservoir's waters, including the four-thousand-year-old remnants of the homeland of the Ba people. The Chinese government feels that despite these problems the completion of such a gigantic project is a source of national pride, and its contribution of such a huge amount of clean, renewable energy is immensely important.

Although it is not renewable, a switch from coal to gas brings instantly cleaner air. In Beijing, a massive effort has been made to switch from coal boilers to gas boilers for heating to try and clean the city's filthy air in time for the Olympics. Since the early years of the twenty-first century, China has begun to develop gas reserves found in the Tarim basin in Xinjiang in the west of the country. The region is very remote, so delivering the gas where it is needed is a challenge. To supply Shanghai with gas, the 3,900-kilometre (2,400-mile) west–east pipeline was laid over incredibly tricky mountain terrain. In 2005 this began supplying gas to Shanghai's power stations, and by 2010 it is hoped all Shanghai's power will be gas generated. In 2008, a gas pipeline almost twice as long will carry gas from Xinjiang to Guangdong in the south.

Failed initiatives

Since 1998, SEPA has been central to the Chinese government's efforts to deal with environmental problems and its influence can be seen in many environmental initiatives. The problem is that it doesn't have quite the staff or the power to deliver all its plans. China's tenth five-year-plan starting in 2000, for instance, called for a 10 per cent reduction in sulphur dioxide emissions. By 2005, sulphur dioxide emissions had actually gone up by 27 per cent.

WATER MAP

In November 2006, a Chinese non-governmental organisation called the Institute of Public and Environmental Affairs unveiled a striking new map. It showed the effects of water pollution in China in graphic and shocking detail. The *China Water Pollution Map*, the brainchild of green activist Ma Jun, was compiled using government data, and its appearance was a clear sign of how much more willing the government now is to acknowledge the extent of the problems.

The map not only ranks towns and regions by just how polluted they are, but also by how transparent local officials are about the problem. Even more surprisingly, it names and shames the enterprises responsible for the worst pollution. Eighty of the 5,500 companies named were European and American multinationals such as Pepsi and General Motors. If companies want their name removed from the map, they must agree to a third-party environmental audit. By July 2007, some thirty companies had responded to being named, mostly the multinationals, and six had agreed to an audit or gone even further, such as Panasonic Battery, which refitted its Shanghai plant with a water-treatment system. Ma Jun believes that multinationals are more sensitive to public pressure because of their big brand names, so to put pressure on the domestic enterprises, he plans to target the multinationals they supply such as Wal-Mart and IBM. Ma Jun's next project is an air-quality map.

The big problem is that although China now has whole raft of environmental regulations, SEPA and other organisations have very little real power to impose them at a local level. Factory owners are often protected by their contacts with local party officials. Many officials turn a blind eye as factories build secret pipes to discharge chemicals into rivers, or release airborne toxins at night. An inspection of 529 plants along the Yellow River in 2007 showed that 44 per cent had violated environmental laws. Almost half the 75 water-treatment works along the river were completely useless. Yet SEPA can do almost nothing about it. SEPA's branches around the country, known as Environmental Protection Bureaus (EPBs), are largely in the hands of local governments, which are pressed to maintain growth and employment in their area. It's quite common for an EPB to fine an enterprise for an environmental breach, only for them to hand the money on to the local government, which then gives it back to the enterprise as a tax break.

Even when SEPA does manage to close a filthy factory down, the factories simply pick up and move to a poorer area where local officials are so concerned about jobs and tax revenues that they will put up with pollution. This is what was behind the sudden shift a few years ago of paper and chemical plants, which need lots of water, from coastal Jiangsu to landlocked and poor Jiangxi.

Despite all these problems, China's current leaders at least seem determined to address them. In contrast to past attitudes, they have been much more open about acknowledging the problems. They have tried to give environmental legislation more teeth, and have requested local governments to conduct environmental impact assessment studies before embarking on new projects. In 2006, too, they introduced the idea of a 'green GDP', which factors environmental costs into calculations of economic growth. That way, they felt, the green issues would not continually get swept aside by the drive for economic progress – both at national and local level. Their first estimate suggested that treating pollution cost US$116 billion in 2004 – nearly 5 per cent of GDP. Most feel that is a huge underestimate of the real costs, but it was at least a step in the right direction.

CHAPTER 5   CHINA AND THE WORLD

'Therefore one hundred victories in one hundred battles is not the most skillful. Seizing the enemy without fighting is the most skillful.'

Sun Tzu, *The Art of War* [6th century BCE]

In November 2006, Beijing underwent a sudden transformation. Factories were closed down to ensure the air was clear. Half a million cars were banned from the city centre to ensure traffic flowed smoothly. Giant hoardings were put up to hide the worst eyesores, and were painted with vast pictures of animals – zebras, giraffes, elephants. Flowerbeds were rolled out. Trees were planted. Huge slogans were painted saying, 'Friendship, peace, co-operation and development.' In some ways, it seemed like a dress rehearsal for the 2008 Olympics, yet this was far more than a rehearsal. Although it received scant attention in the western media, this was a huge event in China. Beijing was playing host to the heads of 48 African governments.

For all the well-publicised statements of intent of the western governments to free Africa from poverty, none of them had ever given African leaders this much attention and put them so clearly in the spotlight for people at home to see. It is no wonder that the Chinese are winning many African hearts and minds. While the western world is busy talking, and treating them like poor children who need nurturing, it seems to some Africans, the Chinese are actually doing something, and treating them, at least superficially, like adults. At the Beijing summit, President Hu promised to double aid to Africa by 2009 and provide US$5 billion in loans and credits, to train fifteen thousand African professionals and set up a fund for building schools and hospitals. More importantly, the Beijing summit focused on two thousand trade deals with Africa, to boost China–Africa trade. With US$42 billion-worth of trade in 2006, China has already replaced the USA as Africa's leading trading partner.

China's resources quest

On the surface at least, China's courting of Africa has a clear intent. China needs resources to sustain its economic growth and Africa has them. Their main target has been oil from the Sudan, Angola, Equatorial Guinea, Gabon and Nigeria, but they also want platinum from Zimbabwe, copper from Zambia, tropical timber from Congo-Brazzaville and iron ore from South Africa. And it's not just Africa that China has been courting. Through the whole of his presidency, George W Bush has not spent more than about a week in neighbouring South America. Yet in 2004, President Hu Jintao spent over two weeks there, assiduously talking with South American governments and pledging billions of dollars of investment in Argentina, Brazil, Chile, Venezuela, Bolivia and Cuba. This pattern has continued and the Chinese leaders, once thought of as being somewhat isolationist, have gone on a charm offensive around the world. In 2006, for instance, Premier Wen Jiabao went to fifteen different countries, while President Hu visited Russia, Saudi Arabia, Morocco, Nigeria, Kenya, India and Pakistan, not to mention Vietnam where he met most Asian leaders, the Beijing African summit and a major visit to the USA.

Almost unnoticed, too, by the western world, which has had its attention focused firmly on the Middle East, China has been extending its trading links with its neighbours in such a way that it is set to replace the USA as the dominant force in South-east Asia. While American trade with the region has stayed pretty static for most of the twenty-first century so far, China's has been racing away. And it's not simply money that is being exchanged. In northern Thailand, Chinese engineers have blasted away the rapids on the Mekong River so that large boats can gain access to Chinese factories there. Chinese construction companies are building motorways to link Kunming in China to Hanoi in Vietnam, Mandalay in Burma and Bangkok in Thailand.

Of course, it is resources that are the driving force behind these overtures, which is why Australia, too, is being drawn into China's expanding friendship circle. But in 2006, Hu made a friendly visit to India, a country it went to war with in 1962, and pledged to double trade and to bid jointly for oil developments on which both nations had previously been competing. Then in spring 2007, Premier Wen paid a remarkably cordial visit to China's *bête noire*, Japan, and the real possibility of some kind of detente between these two old enemies seemed possible (see Chapter 8, China and Japan).

Peaceful rise?

All of this seems to fit with China's intention of keeping its prosperity growing to lift its people out of poverty without making any ripples in the world – an intention famously described by Zheng Bijian, chair of the China Reform Forum as a 'peaceful rise'. After Tiananmen (see pages 63–66), Deng Xiaoping advised that China should 'observe developments soberly, maintain our position, meet challenges calmly, hide our capacities and bide our time, remain free of ambition, never claim leadership.' Deng felt that China should never throw its weight around, threaten its neighbours nor disturb world peace. All the signs are that this is the policy that China has pursued in relation to the world over the last decade. When the Americans accidentally bombed the Chinese embassy in Belgrade in the former Yugoslavia in 1999, the Chinese allowed a brief upsurge of public protest, but quickly damped it down. They did the same in 2001, when an American spy plane collided with a Chinese fighter over Chinese territory, killing the pilot.

Politically, China's attitude seems to be to keep itself to itself – and it expects other countries to do likewise. That is why it brooks no interference on the issue of Tibet, which it regards as a purely internal matter. The same goes for Taiwan (see Chapter 6). For the same reason, China was quietly disturbed by the NATO intervention in Yugoslavia in 1999. It was also dead against foreign intervention in Iraq and Afghanistan.

African strings

It is this non-interventionist stance that has allowed China to enter into trading links with African countries, for instance, without looking too closely at their internal politics. The problem with this is that it is beginning to bring it into, perhaps unanticipated, conflict. While the West often extends aid or loans in Africa only to regimes it is happy with, or providing certain conditions are met, China appears to offer money with no questions asked and no strings attached – which is very appealing to some African leaders, but causes anxiety in the West, especially among human-rights organisations. In 2004, when the International Monetary Fund held up a loan to Angola because of suspected corruption, the Chinese stumped up US$2 billion instead. Similarly, while the West has been trying to isolate President Robert Mugabe in Zimbabwe, the Chinese have stepped in with US$2 billion dollars worth of loans, not to mention Chinese arms. And when the African Union expelled François Bozizé of the Central African Republic after a violent coup, China gave him a huge loan and invited him to China.

It is the Sudan, however, that has been the biggest bone of contention. Sudan has become a focus of international concern because of the ethnic slaughter in the Darfur region, where 200,000 people have died and 2.5 million have been forced out of their homes. Yet apparently heedless of the Darfur situation and the moves in the rest of the world to impose sanctions, China helped build a pipeline to develop Sudan's oil resources and now takes two-thirds of the country's oil. Sudan's president Omar al-Bashir's fabulous new palace is being built courtesy of an interest-free loan from China. What upset critics most, though, was that China used its position on the UN Security Council to dilute resolutions pressuring the Sudan government to allow a UN force in to protect the people of Darfur. When questioned about China's attitude in 2006, Foreign Minister Zhou Wenzhong said, 'Business is business. We try to separate politics from business, and in any case the internal position of Sudan is an internal affair, and we are not in a position to influence them' (quoted in Will Hutton's *The Writing on the Wall* (2007)).

China yields

The chorus of international pressure on China over Darfur has grown more intense, and there are signs that the Chinese are responding. In April 2007, the Chinese sent a special envoy to persuade Sudanese president Omar al-Bashir to accept the UN peacekeeping force, and by June the pressure had worked. This is not enough for some, however, since it is Chinese weapons that are being used against victims in Darfur. Pressure from US politicians, Hollywood stars such as Mia Farrow and human-rights groups has pushed China to go further, but China argues that its softly, softly approach is working – and that it is more than willing to co-operate. At a news conference in May 2007, Chinese foreign ministry spokeswoman Jiang Yu insisted, 'I can say that on the Darfur issue, China and the United States have the same goal. We hope to solve the issue by political means, so we are ready to make joint efforts with the international community, including the US.' Yet the negative publicity over Darfur continued in the run-up to the Beijing Olympics, as film director Steven Spielberg resigned as the Games' artistic director.

As China is beginning to learn, it cannot engage economically with the rest of the world without engaging politically. In Africa, moreover, they are coming up against criticism not just for the unsavoury governments they are willing to deal with, but also their own behaviour. On the one side is the trading pattern in which, some say, China takes Africa's resources, then floods it with cheap products and even food that make it impossible for Africans to compete. In December 2006, South African president Thabo Mbeki warned Africa that it must not allow China to become like one of the old colonial powers. On the other, Chinese rigs and mining operations in Africa are acquiring a reputation for poor safety, exploitative wages and job insecurity.

International alignment

So far, under Hu and Wen, China has been playing its hand remarkably well, and allaying many of the fears people had about the country in the Mao era. Indeed, an international poll in 2005 of opinions of the public around the world by the US-based Pew Research Center found that China is far more popular and trusted around the world than the USA is. Despite the criticism over its dealings with unsavoury regimes, and its trading practices, China has successfully kept a low profile, and has generally done the 'right thing' when necessary. In the 1950s, China went to war against the USA to protect North Korea and lost millions of soldiers, but when North Korea conducted its nuclear test in autumn 2006, China not only joined the USA in condemning Kim Jong-il, but supported the UN resolution imposing sanctions on North Korea.

On the other hand, China's interests in maintaining stability in the region are clear with North Korea. That isn't the case with Iran. China has refused to back the tough sanctions against Iran that Europe and America want to use to halt Iran's nuclear programme. It may be that the Chinese believe the Iranians should be left to develop nuclear power in peace, as it is, but there is no doubt that China wants Iranian oil and gas, and has signed a US$16 billion contract for it.

As China's economy expands, and it extends its global reach, it will find itself not only exposed to more and more pressures like those it has faced over Darfur and Zimbabwe. It will also find that its impact on the world may bring animosity in places it doesn't always expect.

Trade wars?

One area of potential conflict is trade and finance. The USA already has a massive trade imbalance with China – in fact, the biggest in history. In 2005, the USA imported US$240 billion of goods from China and exported back just US$40 billion. Over the next few years, that trading deficit is likely to increase. The only reason it is sustainable is that China is happy to put its entire surplus into dollars.

American manufacturers, and many American workers, are unhappy with this surplus, as are politicians who worry about this dependence. They complain that they are being

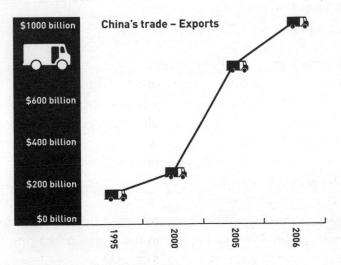

Source: PRC General Administration of Customs

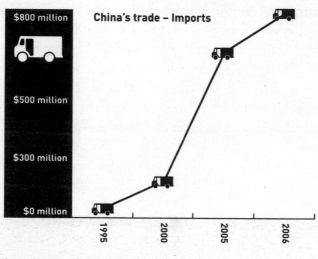

China's trade – Imports

$800 million

$500 million

$300 million

$0 million

1995   2000   2005   2006

Source: PRC General Administration of Customs

unfairly undercut by Chinese factories and that the American market is being continually swamped by the dumping of cheap Chinese products. Six American industries – textiles, clothes, wooden furniture, colour TVs, semiconductors and shrimping – have already won special tariff protections against China. The pressure for more is building up, with Democrats making a noise about both the loss of American jobs and China's record on human rights. More and more Congressmen are drafting anti-China legislation, from putting up trade barriers to getting China suspended from the World Trade Organization.

If any of the more severe measures actually gets through, it is likely to have dramatic impact. At the very least, China will turn its economic power on Europe instead, where the China effect has so far been small – though there has already been opposition in Europe to any increase in Chinese imports – with potentially devastating effects on jobs and businesses in Europe. At worst, it could provoke the Chinese to give up on the dollar for their vast foreign reserves, provoking an economic meltdown worse than the 1930s, as America's finances collapse.

| China's Top Export Destinations 2006 ($ billion) | | | |
Rank	Country	Volume	% Change*
01	United States	203.5	24.9
02	Hong Kong	155.4	24.8
03	Japan	91.6	9.1
04	South Korea	44.5	26.8
05	Germany	40.3	23.9
06	The Netherlands	30.9	19.3
07	United Kingdom	24.2	27.3
08	Singapore	23.2	39.4
09	Taiwan	20.7	25.3
10	Italy	16.0	36.7

*Per cent change over 2005
Source: PRC General Administration of Customs, China's Customs Statistics

China's Top Import Suppliers 2006 ($ billion)			
Rank	Country	Volume	% Change*
01	Japan	115.7	15.2
02	South Korea	89.8	16.9
03	Taiwan	87.1	16.6
04	United States	59.2	21.8
05	Germany	37.9	23.3
06	Malaysia	23.6	17.3
07	Australia	19.3	19.3
08	Thailand	18.0	28.4
09	Russia	17.7	37.3
10	Singapore	17.7	7.0

*Per cent change over 2005
Source: PRC General Administration of Customs, China's Customs Statistics

BRITAIN'S CHINA BOOM

Britain has not suffered much from the China effect, yet. Indeed, if anything, China's boom has given Britain quite a comfortable ride in the last decade. Some jobs have been lost to cheap Chinese competition, such as those at Rover cars, but often these were in industries that were close to the edge anyway. On the other hand, wages at the bottom of the scale have been kept low, and so too has the price of manufactured goods. This means that inflation and interest rates have stayed low, fuelling soaring property prices. With interest rates low and property prices rising, British consumers have felt comfortable borrowing against the equity in their homes or simply on credit to spend at an unprecedented level. All this spending has created more jobs in retail, services and a whole raft of industries that rely on personal consumption.

Oil wars

Many people believe that oil production is now at a peak – as high as it will ever be. Although new oilfields are still being found and developed, they cannot compensate for the fall-off in production from existing fields as they begin to run out. Not everyone agrees, but oil consumption around the world is still climbing, and in China it is rising faster than anywhere else. In 2003, China shot past Japan to become the world's second largest oil consumer after the USA, and since then it has accounted for 40 per cent of the total growth in global demand for oil. If current trends continue, China will overtake the USA in 209 years – even though the USA's consumption is still rising. So just where is all this oil going to come from?

On the whole, China has been remarkably careful to avoid competing with the western world too strongly. That's why it's willing to take Iranian oil, and has played a key part in developing fields away from the Middle East in Africa, especially Sudan and Angola, and South America. These may not prove sufficient, and if the USA gets into hostilities with Iran, China may be forced to take sides, or lose a vital source of oil.

Military build-up

Over the last decade, according to London's International Institute for Strategic Studies, China's military spending has tripled, and seems to be accelerating. In 2006 alone, Chinese spending on arms grew by 15 per cent. For a country that insists that it is rising peacefully, this seems an odd contradiction, and people have begun to wonder just what this arms build-up is for. Some believe it is aimed at Taiwan, and begin to ask the question, what would America do if China attacked Taiwan? Could this be the start of a superpower war? Most believe this is unlikely since it is in both China's and the USA's interests to maintain the status quo in Taiwan (see Chapter 6).

It could just be, though, that China is building up its forces to the point where the USA will decide the cost of intervention to save Taiwan is simply too high. That's what some American hawks say. The aim of the spending has turned the mass numbers of the PLA (People's Liberation Army) into a smaller, nimbler but technologically advanced force that can operate at the same level as American forces. Its navy also has cruise and other anti-ship missiles designed to pierce the electronic defences of US ships. All the same, Chinese military spending is just a tenth of American spending, and even less than British spending, so it seems unlikely to be able to sustain a serious war against the USA, even if it wanted to. So a war over Taiwan seems unlikely.

If the Chinese weapons are not for Taiwan, what else could they be for? It may be simply defensive security. Twice in the twentieth century, China was invaded – the last time with devastating effects. It also has land frontiers 22,000 kilometres (13,670 miles) long and a coast 18,000 kilometres (11,185 miles) long, which need protecting. It may also be that China is anticipating a conflict over resources. It has already sent its navy out in a war of wills with Japan over disputed oilfields.

Democratic future?

At the moment, China seems to be content to play a low-key role in the world. A poll conducted in China in 2006 showed that 87 per cent of Chinese people thought their country should take a greater role in world affairs and should soon match that of the USA. The Chinese were probably thinking of pride in their country, and their growing belief that they should occupy their 'rightful place' in the world rather than seeking to dominate the world in any imperialistic sense. The problem is that their rightful place could be at other people's expense. Moreover, China remains a one-party state, which often suppresses dissidence, and so far it has not been choosy about the states with which it fraternises. Over the last twenty years the number of democracies in the world has doubled so that two-thirds of the world's nations are now democracies. It is just possible that China's rise may see this swing towards democracy slow or even decline – unless, of course, China itself moves towards democracy.

CHAPTER 6   CHINA AND TAIWAN

'Taiwan is an inalienable part of China's territory. The greatest threat to peace in the Taiwan Straits is from the splitist activities by the "Taiwan Independence" forces.'
Chinese President Hu Jintao, 2003

In June 2007, Taiwan was deeply hurt by a small country right across the world, Costa Rica. It turned out that Costa Rica, one of the few countries that officially recognise Taiwan, had switched allegiance and decided to support the People's Republic of China instead. It seemed that the Costa Ricans could no longer resist the lure and financial blandishments of increasingly prosperous – and big – mainland China. Costa Rica's president Oscar Arias explained it very simply as 'an act of elemental realism'. Taiwan's foreign minister James Huang was upset, replying, 'This is not something that a country that stands for peace and democracy should do, cut ties with its partner of 60 years.' Unfortunately for Taiwan, it seems likely that more of the island's dwindling band of supporters, such as Panama and Nicaragua, will follow suit. The score now stands at mainland China 170, Taiwan 24 – and most of Taiwan's team is small and poor.

It's all very different from the 1950s, when the situation was completely reversed – and all the more ironic since Taiwan is now a fully functioning democracy, whereas back then it was a military dictatorship under the rule of General Chiang Kai-shek. Chiang Kaishek, the leader of China's nationalists the Guomindang (GMD), had fled to the island of Taiwan after his armies were defeated by the Communists in 1948. There he was joined by up to two million of his followers. Chiang's followers are called Mainland Chinese to distinguish them from most other people in Taiwan who also came originally from the mainland, mainly from Fujian and Guangdong, but long ago in imperial times. There are also small numbers of Taiwan aborigines.

The Chiang gang

When they arrived in 1949, Chiang and his followers – essentially the Chinese Nationalist army – quickly took control of the island and set up China's National Assembly here. For Chiang and the GMD their stay on Taiwan was always meant to be short-term. The People's Republic of China (PRC) established by the Communists on the mainland was, as far as Chiang was concerned, illegitimate, and it was only a matter of time before he and his followers returned to the mainland to re-establish the Republic of China (ROC). Taiwan was for him only a province of the ROC, even though over the years, people have come to talk of Taiwan as the Republic of China and mainland China as the People's Republic of China. The PRC, meanwhile, likewise claims that Taiwan is a province, but a province of the PRC, not the ROC.

Until 1971, it was the Communists who were regarded by the rest of the world as the renegades, and the ROC were regarded as China's only legitimate Chinese government. But the efforts of the PRC's Zhou Enlai to gain international recognition – along with US president Richard Nixon's attempt to woo China as a counterbalance to the Soviet Union – finally paid off. The UN switched diplomatic recognition to the PRC, not the ROC, which was ejected from the UN. Since then, the number of countries recognising the ROC has dwindled. The ROC maintains diplomatic links with most countries in a non-official way, however, through agencies rather than ambassadors.

Taiwan grows up

Relations between mainland China and Taiwan have always been fraught, and China always threatened to retake Taiwan from the GMD by force if necessary. Throughout the 1960s and 1970s, though, Taiwan began to develop into a hugely prosperous, dynamic country – with a booming economy that made it one of the Four Asian Tigers (along with Hong Kong, Singapore and South Korea). Taiwan's prosperity was no doubt helped by the fact that the GMD had brought with them from mainland China all China's gold reserve and foreign currency. Yet although it was becoming a modern state economically and industrially, it was still a military dictatorship under the control of Chiang Kaishek and the GMD. Effectively, Taiwan was ruled by the Mainland Chinese, who form just 14 per cent of the island's population.

In 1975, however, Chiang died and was succeeded by his son Chiang Ching-ko, and the mood began to change. In 1984 Chiang junior made the bold choice of someone outside the GMD, native Taiwanese Lee Teng-hui, as his vice-president. A few years later a party calling for democratic rule and Taiwan independence, the Democratic Progressive Party (DPP), was set up and, although banned, was tolerated. Then in 1987, Chiang Ching-Ko lifted martial law.

Once Chiang Ching-Ko died in 1988, the process of democratisation began to gather pace as Lee Teng-hui became president. Significantly, though, it was not simply a process of democratisation, as Lee Teng-hui began to make a fundamental shift in Taiwan's relationship to China. He began to abandon the pretence that Taiwan's government was just a government in waiting, ready to take over the whole of China. Instead, he shifted the focus to Taiwan alone. Instead of being issued by the Provincial Bank of Taiwan (implying Taiwan was just a province of China), bank notes were issued by the Central Bank of Taiwan, for instance. More dramatically, Lee got rid of the old Chinese National Assembly, which still had the same members as when it was elected by all of China in 1947 – except those who had died of old age, of course. In 1996, Lee was elected president by Taiwan's first democratic elections. Then, in 2000, the GMD were booted out as Chen Shui-ban of the DPP was elected as the head of the first non-GMD government. In 2004, Chen Shui-ban was elected for a second term at the head of a DPP-led coalition called the Pan-Greens, which favours proper independence for Taiwan. The opposing GMD-led Pan-Blue coalition favours eventual reunification with China.

Dire straits

All of these developments posed a dilemma for the Chinese. After decades of hostility, relations between China and Taiwan had begun to improve in the 1980s. Deng Xiaoping had even proposed the 'one-state, two systems' solution, which was applied to Hong Kong and Macau. Under this, Taiwan would be part of the PRC but would be allowed some degree of autonomy and allowed to maintain its own government. In the early 1990s, President Lee unofficially renounced the ROC's claim over mainland China, though it remains in Taiwan's constitution. To the casual observer, this might seem a conciliatory move, but the PRC were worried. While the ROC still claimed China, there was a tacit assumption on both sides that they both were simply opponents in China's civil war and that Taiwan was just a province of China. The renunciation of the ROC's claim to mainland China was a clear move to separate Taiwan from China – the last thing China wanted.

When Taiwan moved towards democratic elections in 1996, China was so disturbed that it began conducting military exercises near Taiwan and fired several 'test' missiles over the island in an attempt to intimidate Lee into cancelling the elections. Immediately, President Bill Clinton ordered the biggest display of US naval power since the Korean War, sending two aircraft carriers to the Taiwan Straits to send a clear message to the Chinese. The possibility of a nuclear war between China and the USA frightened everyone back to their senses. Ruffled feathers were smoothed and the Taiwanese went ahead with their election. All the Chinese sabre-rattling had done was boost Lee's support in Taiwan and ensure he was elected.

AMERICAN FRIENDS

There is no doubt that the USA is Taiwan's most coveted friend and has been since the connection was forged during the Second World War and the Cold War, when the USA was very pro-Chiang Kaishek as a buttress against communism. It was a real test of their friendship, therefore, when the USA withdrew diplomatic recognition from Taiwan in the 1970s and transferred it to China. Despite this slap in the face for Taiwan, the Americans were unwilling to abandon it altogether and the US Congress passed the Taiwan Relations Act in 1979, which undertook to supply Taiwan with defensive weapons, and to consider any attack on Taiwan as of 'great concern' to the USA.

Just how seriously they meant that was demonstrated in 1996, when President Clinton dispatched the US navy to Taiwan in response to China's provocative missile tests. All the same, it was clear that the Americans did not want to commit themselves too far, as Clinton two years later pledged the USA would stand by 'three no's' – no to Taiwanese independence, no to China splitting in two and no to Taiwan joining any organisation that required being recognised as a state for entry (i.e. the UN). The Bush administration has perhaps been a little more hawkish. The BBC has quoted an unnamed US official briefing from 2003 that says, 'The president did tell the Chinese in no uncertain terms that we would have to get involved if China tried to use coercion or force to unilaterally change the status of Taiwan.' But there is no doubt that the USA walks a diplomatic tightrope when it comes to Taiwan. It has no wish to upset China at all, especially as China's growing prosperity accelerates trade links between the two countries. But neither is it willing to abandon Taiwan altogether. The result is that there is a lot of play on semantics. The USA 'acknowledges' rather than 'recognises' – that is, endorses – China's claim that Taiwan is part of China. It also 'does not support' rather than 'opposes' the idea of Taiwanese independence. It remains unambiguous, however, in its insistence that the situation should be resolved peacefully.

What's in a name?

Since then, Taiwan has tried to re-enter the UN – this time in its own right, rather than as representative for the whole of China as it had been when it was ejected in 1971. Under Lee, the ROC called itself the 'Republic of China on Taiwan'. Chen Shui-bian took it a little further, calling it in his first term 'Republic of China (Taiwan)'. Since he was re-elected in 2004, he has been saying that Taiwan should rejoin the UN under the name 'Taiwan'. Since it is not recognised as a sovereign nation, it would only join as an observer at first, like the Palestinians, but, of course, most people would see it as a step on the road to independent statehood. That's exactly how the PRC see it, of course, and it is determined to block Taiwan's re-entry to the UN. With China on the Security Council with a veto it is unlikely that Taiwan will make much progress.

Interestingly, though, that is just the way most Taiwanese probably like it. While support for the GMD and the idea of reunification even among the Mainland Chinese has dwindled, only a minority of Taiwanese people actually support Chen and the Pan-Greens' line of full independence. Most just want to be left to get on with their increasingly prosperous lives in peace, without upsetting their powerful neighbours. While polls show that two-thirds of Taiwanese would fight for their country if the Chinese tried to take them over, just 14 per cent wish to up the ante by making Taiwan fully independent. For the wealthier Taiwanese at least, the status quo is fine.

Money talks

There are good reasons for the pragmatic line taken by Taiwan, apart from the sheer size and military might of their mainland neighbours. In fact, over the last twenty years, people in Taiwan have been forging closer and closer ties with the mainland. After Hong Kong, Taiwan has been the biggest investor in the growing Chinese economy. Since the late 1980s, Taiwanese businesses have pumped over US$100

TAIWAN SLIPS

Knowing just what to call Taiwan has become something of a nightmare. Even those to whom it really matters occasionally slip up and get things wrong. The online encyclopedia Wikipedia lists a whole string of gaffes by politicians. Both US presidents Reagan and Bush, of course, have been right in there with the slips of the tongue, wrongly referring to Taiwan as a country, which, of course, in the official US view it isn't. Donald Rumsfeld went even further, describing Taiwan in 2005 as a 'sovereign nation'. But it isn't just the Americans. PRC Premier Zhu Rongji accidentally described mainland China and Taiwan as two countries, while when Lien Chan and the GMD visited Beijing in 2005, they were introduced by the PRC as one of Taiwan's political parties even though they were trying to negotiate with the GMD on the basis that they both saw China as a whole including Taiwan. And in February 2007, apparently, the Royal Grenada Police Band (from the Caribbean island of Grenada) played the Taiwanese national anthem to welcome a delegation from the PRC who had funded the reconstruction of a local stadium!

billion dollars into the mainland. It's not just money the Taiwanese have put on China; more than a million of them actually work there. Although no one knows for sure, 40 to 80 per cent of China's electronics exports probably come from Taiwanese-owned factories, and a huge proportion of Taiwan's exports go to China.

TAIWAN'S ELECTRONIC MASTERY

The key to Taiwan's prosperity has been the island's astonishing success in the high-tech industry. With a population of just 23 million, Taiwan has come to dominate the IT business to an extraordinary degree. If you own a personal computer, a notebook computer or an iPod, or watch DVDs on an LCD screen, you can almost guarantee that the Taiwanese have had a hand in producing it. China is coming to rival Taiwan as an IT supplier, but it's the Taiwanese who are often supplying the brains or the money behind the Chinese companies. Very few of Taiwan's IT companies are yet household names, but they are suppliers to most of the familiar global brands. Stretched out along Taiwan's west coast are outfits such as: Asustek Computer, which owns the Chinese factories that make iPods and Apple mini computers; AU Optronics, which makes Sony's PlayStation; Quanta, which is the world's leading notebook computer maker; and Taiwan Semiconductor Manufacturing Co, which makes more chips than any other company. A decade ago, Taiwan's IT business made its money mainly by supplying dirt-cheap components or machines designed elsewhere. Now,

---

however, Taiwan has upped its game, getting the cheap manufacture done in China and becoming a key innovator itself. The government has been a key player, funding initiatives such as the Industrial Technology Research Institute in Hsinchu. The result is that the Taiwanese have a wealth of IT talent together with a degree of flexibility in responding to corporate custom-made orders that has kept them one step ahead of the competitors.

In a remarkable turnaround considering their past enmity, the GMD, with the support of many Taiwanese businessmen, have begun to get quite pally with the PRC in a bid to paint Chen and the DPP as extremist separatists. In April 2005, Lien Chan, then leader of the GMD, made a hugely publicised visit to Beijing, and millions of Taiwanese and Chinese watched live on TV as Lien Chan was entertained in a lavish state reception by China's President Hu Jintao. Lien Chan came back to Taiwan not only with two giant pandas for Taipei zoo but also a warm reception from many of Taipei's business elite.

The PRC, of course, are very much aware of their hold on Taiwanese business and, as well as wooing the GMD, they have been leaning on businesses that are seen as pro-Chen, and favouring those who are pro-China. Just before Lien Chan went to Beijing, Chen was stunned to find an open letter from an old supporter Hsu Wen-long in a Taipei newspaper criticising Chen's push for independence as a recipe for disaster. Hsu Wen-long's Chi Mei group has a lot of business in China and was keen to expand. According to the Taiwanese government, the Chinese applied a lot of pressure on Hsu.

Softening line

Over the past few years, Chen has been taking a more and more conciliatory line. All the same, support for him and a strong independence stance have been dwindling. In May 2007, the DPP voted for Frank Hsieh as their candidate for the 2008 presidential elections and rejected Chen's choice, the current prime minister Su Tseng-chang. While Su favours a tough attitude to China, Frank Hsieh takes a far softer line. The switch didn't work for voters, though, for the GMD's candidate Ma Ying-jeou has stayed ahead in the polls. It seems likely that whoever wins, Taiwan will do its best not to antagonise China.

All this is very well, but the problem remains that Taiwan's status is still ambiguous. While many Taiwanese are quite comfortable with the ambiguity, it is fraught with dangers. China's attitude is still that Taiwan is part of China, and that indeed is the internationally recognised official situation. Moreover, the Chinese retain the right to use force should Taiwan move towards independence. On the other hand, although many Taiwanese have close ties with China, an increasing number feel they are Taiwanese, not Chinese. And even those who are pro-unification, such as the GMD, will not accept Chinese overtures until there is some move towards democracy. Both sides are heavily armed, and those arms are pointed towards each other across the narrow Taiwan Straits. There is no doubt who would win if it came to an armed conflict. All that remains open is how long the Taiwanese could hold out. Some say up to a month; others say just six minutes.

Would the USA come to Taiwan's rescue and, if so, could it come in time? Most observers pray these questions will never need to be answered, but while relations between China and Taiwan are better now than they have ever been, it is far from a foregone conclusion that they will not.

CHAPTER 7   HONG KONG ON SONG?

'It used to be said that no one ever made money out of betting against Hong Kong. That remains true today, and it will still be the case in 2017.'

Lord Chris Patten, *Guardian*, 30 June 2007

On 1 July 2007, the people of Hong Kong went out to enjoy the lavish celebrations to mark the tenth anniversary of the handover of the city from Britain to China, and things were looking much, much better for Hong Kong than most people thought possible when the handover took place on a rainy day in 1997. The Hong Kong economy is booming and property prices, always a sign of financial well-being to Hong Kongers, are at an all-time high.

To add to the sense of optimism (for property owners at least), an interesting piece of news reached the ears of the protestors taking part in the annual democracy rally who are demanding full democratic rights for Hong Kong citizens. The news was that while speaking at the celebrations, Chinese President Hu Jintao said that progress towards political reform – by which it was clear he meant democracy – must happen in a 'gradual and orderly' way. There was no definite date set, but it was the first time the Chinese leadership had made it plain that there is at least some scope for democracy in Hong Kong.

Hong Kong bounce

Ten years after the British handover, things are looking, on the surface at least, remarkably positive for Hong Kong. Despite fears that rule by communist China would kill the city's financial energy and erode basic liberties, Hong Kong seems better off than it was even in the best colonial days. Indeed, Hong Kong's position as the gateway between the world and the world's fastest growing, (soon to be) biggest economy is proving something of a winner.

When Hong Kong was handed over to China in 1997, it handled almost a quarter of China's trade with the outside world. That proportion has shrunk slightly, but in absolute terms it has swelled enormously because China's economy has been growing so fast. Trade with mainland China has risen fourfold since 1997 to reach US$165 billion. Indeed, overall Hong Kong's trade with the world has swelled by almost 70 per cent in the ten years, while its gross domestic product (GDP) rose 7.5 per cent in 2005 and 6.9 per cent in 2006, bringing it to US$254 billion. This is pretty good going for a city already operating at a high level. Indeed, its GDP per capita is the world's sixth highest at not far short of US$40,000. The level of trading activity in Hong Kong is enormous. Also, besides being Asia's key financial services centre, the city is now the world's third biggest air-cargo hub and the second biggest container port by throughput. And more tourists (now over 25 million) are coming to Hong Kong each year than ever to sample the excitement of its teeming, colourful streets, stunning views and the new Disneyland.

PROFILE: LI KA-SHING

'No, I wasn't lucky. I worked hard to achieve the goals I set myself.'

No one sums up the capacity of Hong Kong for enabling people to make money better than Li Ka-shing. His renowned business acumen has earned him a multi-billion dollar fortune that makes him the richest man in China and the ninth richest man in the world.

Born the son of a lowly teacher in Guangdong, he was forced to flee to Hong Kong at the age of 12 in 1940 to escape the terrible strife in China. In Hong Kong, his encounter with his arrogant uncle's wealth fired him with the desire to become rich to show the world he was worth looking at. He was forced to leave school to work in a plastics factory at the age of 15, when his father died from tuberculosis. But his entrepreneurial flare, determination to do things well and sheer hard work enabled him to break away and start his own plastics company, Cheung Kong industries, at just 21.

From making plastics, Li expanded into real estate and was soon a major player in the Hong Kong market. In 1972, Cheung took over Hutchison Wampoa, and in 1985 Hongkong Electric Holdings Limited. Now Li's business dealings stretch from banking to mobile phones, from making plastics to running airports. Hutchison Wampoa is the world's largest port operator and employs one hundred and fifty thousand people worldwide. It controls both ends of the Panama Canal in South America, as well as ports such as Singapore and Hong Kong, making Li hugely powerful.

Li has been one of the biggest investors in the new China, and seems to have business interests almost everywhere there. Naturally, he is very well connected with the Communist Party leadership, and for a year served as chairman of CITIC (China International Trust and Investment Corporation), the Chinese government's chief investment body. This degree of connection has made some Americans wary of him and his influence, but it probably doesn't bother him that much. He is renowned for his philanthropy, giving away well over a billion dollars, but his donation of $US128 million to Hong Kong's medical school provoked a storm of controversy when it was renamed Li Ka Shing Faculty of Medicine in 2006. Li famously paid $US128 million in ransom to the notorious Hong Kong gangster Cheung Chi Keung, when Li's son Victor Li was kidnapped in 1996.

Painting the town red

All this was never quite expected back amid the rain-lashed gloom of 1 July 1997 when Hong Kong was handed over by the British to China. The whole build-up to the handover had been fraught. The process dated back to 1984, when British Prime Minister Margaret Thatcher had signed the agreement with the Chinese to hand Hong Kong back to China when the British lease expired in 1997. The British, of course, signed the agreement without bothering to consult the people of Hong Kong, but following Deng Xiaoping's 'one country, two systems' formula, it guaranteed Hong Kong's essential economic and political structure, including independent courts and free speech, under a Chinese law called the Basic Law. The Tiananmen Square massacre in 1989, however, shook the people of Hong Kong badly. Was this the regime to which they were being handed over? Half a million Hong Kongers immediately took to the streets in protest at the event. Before the massacre, they sent money, medical supplies and messages of sympathy to the students in the square. Afterwards they queued up in their hundreds to donate blood, and withdrew all their savings from mainland banks.

For the People's Republic of China, the reaction in Hong Kong was, officially, dismissed as confirmation that human rights were simply a western conspiracy to bring the Communist government down. The British, however, had to acknowledge that their failure to give Hong Kong's people any say in the direction of their affairs might have been a mistake. Amazingly, Hong Kong was the only part of the British Empire in which there was no semblance of democracy. Foolishly, the British had decided Hong Kongers were only interested in making money; the protests over Tiananmen proved otherwise. Their problem was how to move towards democracy in Hong Kong without upsetting Beijing. In an article in the *Guardian* in 1992, John Gittings cites a Foreign Office bigwig whose comment beautifully sums up the attitude the British powers-that-be had to the dilemma, 'This talk about political reform is all very well, but how long have we got until 1997? If you've just sold your house, you don't suddenly start redecorating it from top to bottom in a colour which the new owner doesn't like!'

Pattern for democracy

British Prime Minister John Major, however, was impatient with the complacency of the Foreign Office mandarins and in 1992 appointed the more combative Chris Patten as the new Hong Kong governor. Immediately, Patten made it clear things were going to change and used a legal loophole to accelerate the move towards democracy that was only hinted at in the Basic Law. Hong Kongers were delighted, but Beijing was livid, since the plan meant that by the time they took over in 1997, Hong Kong would pretty much have full democratic government.

As Patten pushed on with his democratisation plans, British business interests began to get edgy. Upsetting the Chinese could wreck the enticing prospects of the growing Chinese market. Politicians with business connections, such as Lord Young and Lord Prior, began to lean on Patten to soften his approach. In his biography of Patten, Jonathan Dimbleby quotes Lord Young: 'I think a number of us saw there were opportunities in China on a heroic scale. That we could go back and reclaim the markets that were ours in the last century.' Patten, though, was determined to press on, despite the opposition. Events reached a climax when Michael Heseltine, who was trade minister at the time, led a trade delegation to Beijing in 1995 and came back with US$1.6 billion of orders and the prospect of US$8 billion more – but only with the proviso, Heseltine was told, that the issue of Hong Kong was dealt with in a way that would be more acceptable to the Chinese.

As pressure on Patten to ease up mounted, he issued a 'Back me or sack me' ultimatum to his cabinet colleagues. They relented, and Patten was given the green light to pursue his plans, though not without a fair amount of bad blood that has lingered in Conservative Party veins ever since. Patten planned to manipulate the Basic Law to hugely increase the number of members of the Legislative Council that were effectively elected by ordinary Hong Kongers. When the Chinese demurred at the plan, the British went ahead anyway for the 1995 elections. The Council proved short-lived, and it certainly caused a huge amount of friction with the Chinese who saw the British as hypocritical troublemakers, trying to introduce democracy at the last minute after ruling Hong Kong for 150 years without it. Some people dismiss Patten's initiative as a hollow and provocative gesture that failed when the Chinese abandoned it just two years later. Others believe it was an essential taste of democracy for people deeply worried by the Tiananmen Square massacre.

Chinese takeaway

At midnight on 30 June 1997, Hong Kong was formally handed back to China. Chris Patten spoke of how Britain had given Hong Kong 'the rule of law, clean and light-handed government, the values of a free society' and also the beginnings of representative government. Prince Charles, who was there at the handover, wrote in his diaries about the Great Chinese Takeaway, describing goose-stepping Chinese soldiers and 'the appalling old waxworks' of China's leadership.

Whatever they thought, the Chinese moved in on Hong Kong quickly, sending in the People's Liberation Army at the stroke of midnight and declaring the 1995 Legislative Assembly illegitimate. Hong Kong's chief executive was to be elected by an 800-seat chamber of delegates selected by Beijing. Yet beyond that the Chinese seemed at first to be willing to leave well alone. After all, Hong Kong was a very public stage for China – and it was also a hugely valuable source of finance. The army stayed in their barracks and the party leaders stayed in Beijing. Life in Hong Kong seemed to carry on pretty much as before, except that school children began to be taught in Chinese rather than English.

The morning after

Hong Kong's honeymoon, though, was short-lived. The very moment of the handover, Asia was plunged into a catastrophic financial crisis. On the day after the handover, Thailand ran out of foreign-exchange reserves. Instantly, investors began to pull their money out of other Asian countries. Indonesia, Malaysia and South Korea were first to fall, but Taiwan, the Philippines, Singapore and Hong Kong were soon swept into the maelstrom. Property prices in Hong Kong plummeted and many middle-class Hong Kongers found themselves in disastrous negative equity. It seemed Hong Kong's financial bubble had suddenly burst. And worse was to come.

In January 1999, Hong Kong's Court of Appeal found that children on the Chinese mainland had the right to live in Hong Kong if one of their parents was a Hong Kong citizen. The Hong Kong administration was afraid of floods of mainland Chinese streaming across from Guangdong and asked Beijing to 'reinterpret' the relevant law. Beijing made it clear that they expected the Hong Kong government to order the courts to change the ruling – apparently unaware of the idea that Hong Kong's courts are meant to be independent. Many families were split by the ruling, and the people of Hong Kong began to turn against the city's chief executive Tung Chee-haw, an ex-shipping tycoon. Determined not to be swayed by the whims of Hong Kongers, Beijing put Tung in office for a second term in 2002. When asked if Tung was 'the emperor's choice' by a Hong Kong journalist, Chinese President Jiang Zemin apparently lost his temper and told the press not to be so 'naive'. Tung was duly elected, but found himself increasingly embattled.

Tung-tied

First of all, Tung was thought to have badly mismanaged the crisis over the SARS virus (see box, pages 160–1) by trying to play it down. Then he provoked the wrath of the people of Hong Kong by trying to introduce a new security law called Article 23. Article 23 was the last straw, and half a million people took to the streets in protest on the sixth anniversary of the handover on 1 July 2003, and again a year later. Surprisingly to some, Beijing decided to take a softer line. They not only started to relax restrictions on travel from the mainland cities of Guangzhou, Shanghai and Beijing but also sacked Tung in 2005 and replaced him with an old colonial hand, Donald Tsang.

SARS

Hong Kong's position in China is described as a Special Autonomous Region (SAR) so it seemed the SARS virus was fatally suited to it.

The crisis over the SARS virus began in February 2003. With rumours coming out of Guangdong of deaths from bird flu, a doctor arrived from the Chinese mainland and stayed at Hong Kong's Metropole. It turned out he was already ill with a virus, which he managed to spread to sixteen guests on the same floor. The infected guests included airline crew and within days the infection was racing around the world, with people gravely ill as far apart as Toronto, Frankfurt and Hanoi, among other places.

Doctors were terrified that this was the start of a world-wide pandemic of bird flu and an atmosphere of fear bordering on panic erupted around the world, which turned Hong Kong into a pariah as business trips to the city were cancelled, and those who could leave left. The World Health Organization immediately advised against all travel to China, where it was thought the infection had started. The Chinese, who had been trying to cover it all up, launched a massive public hygiene campaign in Guangdong. Reports say that an astonishing eighty million people were mobilised to disinfect streets and houses. These draconian measures seemed to succeed and the spread of the infection in China seemed to stop.

Elsewhere efforts to contain it gradually made headway and by June 2003 the epidemic seemed to have burned itself out. By this time the infection had been named severe acute respiratory syndrome (SARS) after the terrible symptoms it caused, and it was found not to be bird flu, but a coronavirus, one of the viruses that cause colds. The origin of the SARS virus was eventually traced back to animals in Guangdong, such as the masked civet and the ferret badger, which are used in traditional Chinese medicine – ironically, to ward off flu. Hong Kong was eventually declared free of the infection, but the whole episode was a terrible blow to the former colony's morale.

Donald Tsang served out the remainder of Tung's term and was reselected for a further five-year term in 2007. Although it was clear that Tsang would win because Beijing controls the 800-member electoral commission that elects him, the people of Hong Kong felt they were at least partially included in the process. The televised debate between Tsang and democracy advocate Alain Leong drew one of Hong Kong's biggest ever audiences. Polls show that Tsang has a nearly 80 per cent approval rating among Hong Kongers.

Comeback city

Since the low point in 2003, Hong Kong seems to have bounced back. Beijing felt that dissatisfaction with the political situation would melt away if Hong Kong started to prosper again. So it not only announced the building of a US$2 billion dollar bridge and tunnel to link Hong Kong with the Pearl River Delta, but also set up a trade agreement that gave Hong Kong firms preferential access to the mainland. This was like getting a backstage pass at the best gig in town. Hong Kong was already one of the major investors in China but this favour really got things moving.

By 2005, Hong Kong had invested over US$240 billion in mainland companies and was employing twelve million people in China, mostly in the Pearl River Delta. This privileged access to the world's fastest growing economy was the green light for renewed faith in Hong Kong. The city's GDP at once shot up by well over 8 per cent in 2004. Hong Kong's own Hang Seng stock index went up 22 per cent between mid-2004 and mid-2005. Unemployment, which had reached almost 9 per cent in 2003 dropped to barely 5 per cent in just two years. And property prices started to rise. Now almost no one in Hong Kong has a negative equity situation and the fear is rather that new starters are being priced out of the market. In fact, property prices in the top central district rose a staggering 290 per cent between autumn 2003 and autumn 2006, making Hong Kong one of the priciest city centres in the world.

Today, the future is looking much brighter than anyone imagined possible in 1997, but there remain some doubts. First of all, there is the issue of democracy. China has promised it, but has not said when. There is always the fear that, at very least, Beijing could put the brakes on Hong Kong's economic freedom. At worst, critics worry, there could be another Tiananmen-style crackdown, and now Hong Kong would be beyond international support. But Hong Kong has freedom of speech, independent courts, good policing and efficient administration – indeed, all the requisites of democratic government except the vote. Indeed, while things are going smoothly, many ordinary Hong Kongers are not so impatient about getting it. Donald Tsang argues that bringing in democracy too precipitately could cause the kind of chaos it brought to Russia after *perestroika*, and many agree with him.

Hong Kong or China?

There are other, less tangible, issues between Hong Kong and mainland China. Take identity, for instance. Hong Kong's exuberant, wild entrepreneurial spirit could not at first seem more at odds with the sobriety and authoritarianism of the Beijing government. So, some people ask, is Beijing going to drag Hong Kong down, or could Hong Kong change China? The older generation of Hong Kongers see themselves as Hong Kong first and Chinese second, and are determined not to lose that fierce independence. In June 2007, *Time* magazine quoted Yan Xuetong of Tsinghua University in Beijing: 'The return of Hong Kong to China is just half achieved. Hong Kong is a special place of China, still regarded as a foreign country. Hong Kong has returned in name, but not in substance.'

Interestingly, though, that may change quicker and more smoothly than anyone anticipates. Right now there is a younger generation of Hong Kongers growing up who have known nothing but Chinese rule, and have followed the Chinese curriculum at school. Many of these youngsters are actually proud to be Chinese, looking to the mainland for their culture, not to the English-speaking outside world as their parents did. These young people are happy to see themselves as both Chinese and Hong Kongers. Indeed, most of them speak only Chinese, rather than English. This, some Hong Kong's older generation feel, could pose a problem in the future. Hong Kong's business success, they argue, depends on its ability to act as a gateway to the world beyond China – and in particular on the fluency in English of its business community. If Hong Kongers lose their English, Hong Kong could lose its financial edge. Worse still, they worry, the children are learning Cantonese, not Mandarin, so could find themselves with the worst of both worlds – unable to communicate fluently in either English, which could be used in the wider world, or Mandarin, for use in mainland China. Not surprisingly, there is huge demand for places at private international schools where children are taught in English. But though a few wealthy children may be looking to the old country, Hong Kong's future is Chinese.

CHAPTER 8   CHINA AND JAPAN

'There is a Japanese saying: although the wind blows, the mountain will not move. The development of our relations has gone through tempests and twists and turns, but the foundation of our friendship is unshakeable, like Mount Tai and Mount Fuji.'

Chinese Premier Wen Jiabao addressing the Japanese parliament, 12 April 2007

In April 2007, Premier Wen Jiabao made a remarkable visit to Japan, which the official Chinese media rightly described as 'ice-melting'. It was the first visit by any Chinese leader to Japan for seven years, and came less than eighteen months after relations between Japan and China had hit their lowest point for several decades. While there, Wen went on a deliberate and very effective charm campaign, playing baseball, taking part in a tai-chi session and planting a tomato with a Japanese farmer. When jogging early in the morning in Tokyo's Yoyogi Park, he stopped to shake hands with a fellow jogger and told her she would be warmly welcome if she ever came to Beijing. In Osaka, he met business leaders and politicians informally, and recited a poem he had written to sum up his visit: 'Spring has come. The sun shines brightly. The cherry tree blossoms proudly and the snow and ice have melted.'

The climax of Wen's visit, though, was when he addressed the Japanese parliament, the first time a Chinese leader had ever done so. His tone there was direct but remarkably conciliatory. Over the key issue of the Japanese atrocities in China in 1937, he said, 'Japan's invasions caused tremendous damage to the Chinese. The deep scars left in the hearts of the Chinese people cannot be described.' Yet, then, remarkably, he went on to put the blame for Japanese aggression on an extremist elite, and acknowledged that Japan, too, had endured its own share of suffering. It was ample reward for Shinzo Abe's own gesture of conciliation in visiting Beijing in October 2006, just a fortnight after becoming premier of Japan.

The scars of history

The modern issues between China and Japan date back to the 1894–95 Sino-Japanese war, in which Japan finally emerged from China's shadow to inflict a humiliating defeat on its neighbour and announce its arrival as a world power. In the peace reparations that followed, Japan took Formosa (now known as Taiwan), an act which still rankles, even though

Formosa was handed back after the Japanese defeat at the end of the Second World War.

The greatest bitterness, though, stems from the Japanese invasion of northern China in 1931. After six years tightening its grip on the north, Japanese forces swept south and captured Chiang Kaishek's Nationalist capital of Nanjing. What happened next remains the subject of bitter dispute between Japan and China, at least on an official level, but it seems likely that Japanese soldiers went on a frenzied spree of slaughter, looting and rape, in which over a quarter of a million civilians were killed and twenty thousand women were raped. To make matters worse, tens of thousands of Chinese women were then made part of the Japanese soldiers' 'comfort system'. The Chinese say this meant they were forced to be sex slaves. The official Japanese line from Shinzo Abe is that there is no proof of this, but shortly after Wen Jiabao's visit to Japan, a group of prominent Japanese academics pointed out that there was real evidence that the Chinese women actually were used as sex slaves.

During their occupation of China, the Japanese also tried out biological and chemical weapons, often on prisoners-of-war and civilians. When they finally withdrew in 1945, they are believed to have left nearly three-quarters of a million chemical weapons scattered over China.

Economic rivals

After the Second World War, despite defeat, Japan rose to become the economic powerhouse of Asia, while China, on the winning side, long languished in its shadow. Now, however, China is catching up with Japan very fast, and the two countries will soon be the world's second and third biggest economies.

In some ways, this is good for Japan, since China has now roared past the USA as Japan's biggest market, and biggest supplier of manufactured goods. But they are both very demanding of energy resources. Despite their giant economies, they have very little of their own oil, and they are now coming head to head in rivalry over oil supply. They have already clashed on a deal for Iran's oil. In 2004, they argued over whether a pipeline from Siberian oilfields should end on the coast near Japan, or in China. Japan won.

The real hotspot, though, is oil and gasfields in disputed territory under the East China Sea and in the early years of the twenty-first century the two countries began to square off like two playground bullies. In 2004, a Chinese submarine 'accidentally' ventured into Japanese territorial waters near the Sakishima Islands off Okinawa. Then, in February 2005, Japan took possession of the disputed Diaoyu Islands (known as the Senkaku Islands in Japan), which would effectively give them control over some of the biggest oilfields. A few weeks later, the Chinese warned Japan to withdraw or 'take full responsibility' for any consequences. Japan drew up plans for sending fifty-five thousand troops to the Diaoyu Islands if China moved in. As the two nations bristled, China sent five navy ships, including a guided missile destroyer to another disputed field, the Chunxiao gasfield. Eventually, both sides backed down and withdrew their forces, but the tension was high.

Don't talk about the war

Underlying all this economic and military rivalry, however, is still the bitter issue of the war. Japan feels it has done enough to atone for the damage it caused. It has paid substantial war reparations to China, and provided much of the key investment that kick-started the Chinese economy. It has also issued seventeen formal apologies.

Yet this, for China, is not nearly enough. The Japanese have never really apologised for the massacre at Nanjing, and Japanese Nationalists consistently deny that Chinese women were ever made sex slaves. To rub it in, the Chinese feel, Japanese premiers have made a point of regularly visiting the Japanese shrine at Yasukuni, which glorifies Japan's military past, and contains memorials to a thousand war criminals (including fourteen executed by the Allies for war crimes after the Second World War) as well as two-and-a-half million ordinary Japanese soldiers.

There is no doubt that China is breathing down Japan's neck as the dominant economic power in Asia, but Japan wants to assert itself as a world power. Japan's constitution, set up by the Americans in the wake of the Second World War, specifically forbids Japan from waging war and allows it only maintain an army for self-defence. For Japanese Nationalists, the Constitution left Japan 'castrated'. Their country has now done its time, they feel, and it is ready to become a proper military power again. Japan is also seeking a permanent seat on the UN Security Council like China – an idea the Chinese reject vehemently.

Teaching the past

In 2004 and 2005, these pressures began to build to a head. Japanese Prime Minister Junichiro Koizumi reinterpreted the Japanese constitution to allow Japanese troops to join the Americans in Iraq. At the same time, the conservative news media in Japan began to campaign for revision of the constitution while running articles demonising the growing military might of China.

With the sixtieth anniversary of the massacre looming, however, it was Nanjing that became the focus, and both China and Japan began to wage a publicity war to make their case. In China, the Nanjing memorial hall got a hugely expensive makeover, while a whole raft of programmes began appearing on state TV telling of China's resistance to Imperial Japan. *Hero City*, for instance, told how cities across China 'fought bravely against Japan under the leadership of the Communist Party'.

Meanwhile, in Japan, efforts were being made to control how young people saw the event. A comic series called *The Country is Burning* that showed Chinese corpses in a story about the Japanese invasion was hastily withdrawn after protests from politicians. Then 291 Tokyo teachers were sacked for failing to stand during the national anthem at school enrolment and graduation ceremonies.

What really upset the Chinese, though, was a series of schoolbooks that appeared in Japanese schools. These books were distributed by the nationalist Fushosha Publishing Company and downplayed the Japanese atrocities in China, describing the massacre in Nanjing merely as an 'incident' and omitting the number of Chinese deaths altogether. The books were actually a reissue of books first published in 2001, but then withdrawn after the Japanese government asked for changes in response to protests from China and other Asian countries affected by the Japanese invasions. The requested changes had been made, but they weren't enough for the Chinese. When news of these books reached Beijing, thousands of Chinese people took to the streets in protest, stones were thrown at the Japanese Embassy in Beijing and twenty-five million people signed a petition against Japan's bid for a UN Security Council place. Some people believe the Communist Party orchestrated the protests, but there is no doubt that the Japanese invasion is still a bitter issue in China, at least among the older generation.

Let's talk

With tensions still high, Chinese President Hu Jintao and Japanese Premier Junichiro Koizumi met for the previously scheduled Africa–Asia summit in Jakarta in April 2005. Africa was supposed to be the focus of the talks, but the whole issue of the war dominated the atmosphere. Hu and Koizumi met in private and Koizumi issued another apology about Japan's role in the war. 'Japan through its colonial rule and aggression,' acknowledged Koizumi, 'caused tremendous damage.' It didn't go as far as the Chinese would have liked, but tensions began to simmer down, and the two countries agreed to meet to discuss the issue of the gas and oilfields.

The differences between the two sides over the gas and oilfields proved hard to resolve, and by the beginning of 2006, talks had stalled. The Japanese invited Hu Jintao to come to Japan for talks, but he refused to do so while Koizumi continued to pay regular visits to the Yasukuni shrine. All the same, during the summer of 2006, Hu hinted that he might be willing to come 'if conditions are smoothed out'. It was a just a little opening, and when Shinzo Abe replaced Koizumi as Japanese premier in the autumn, he was quick to make the most of it, taking a trip to Beijing and inviting his counterpart Wen Jiabao to come to Tokyo. Abe had been part of Koizumi's government and, like him, was a visitor to the shrine, but as long as he didn't visit the shrine as premier, Wen, perhaps more open-minded than President Hu, could go to Japan without any loss of face.

Blossoming relations

Interestingly, though, the Chinese told the Japanese that the only time Wen could come would be in April. This is not only the best time for cherry blossom, but also the favourite time for visiting the Yasukuni shrine. Only if Abe wanted to really insult the Chinese could he go to Yasukuni in April – and of course he didn't. Another popular time for visiting Yasukuni is August, which just happened to be when China's defence minister scheduled a visit. And when the two countries agreed on a visit for China's President Hu to Japan in 2008, the only date open in Hu's busy diary was in April.

Wen's visit in April 2007 may have been a turning point in Sino-Japanese relations. Wen's words went down well with the Japanese parliament, and his charm offensive won over quite a few Japanese hearts. As a direct result of the visit, China and Japan began to formalise high-level dialogue on economic co-operation, and they signed a joint agreement to tackle global warming beyond the end of the Kyoto protocol in 2012. The Japanese were invited to contribute their know-how (and investment) to environmental projects and Japanese firms were offered the chance to bid for building in China nuclear-power stations and high-speed rail links, such as that between Beijing and Shanghai. Even more significantly, China agreed to the Japanese proposal that the gas and oilfields should be jointly exploited by both countries. All that remained to decide, apparently, was which fields should be exploited.

As if all this weren't enough, the two countries began to explore the possibilities of setting up hotlines between them to co-ordinate search-and-rescue missions in the Sea of Japan, which lies between them, and hotlines between their navies to avoid accidents between them. There is even a possibility that the Chinese navy might be invited on a friendship visit to Tokyo. Meanwhile, the Chinese government began to clamp down on Chinese websites promoting anti-Japanese sentiments, and began setting up cultural exchange visits for young Chinese and Japanese students. When, in January

2008, dozens of Japanese people fell ill after eating frozen *gyoza* dumplings imported from Japan, some people suggested they were deliberately poisoned. Yet the Chinese were quick to co-operate with Japanese demands for an investigation, and tension was defused.

Despite this outbreak of geniality, the differences between the two countries are far from resolved. In China, for instance, Abe's refusal to acknowledge that Asian girls were sex slaves in the Japanese comfort system of the 1930s still rankles. In Japan, news that China has already begun to drill for oil in the Chunxiao field ahead of agreements is bound to cause tension. Moreover, the political reputations of Abe and Wen are on the line. If Abe makes another visit to the Yakasuni shrine, Wen will look like a sucker. Yet Abe, in turn, may come under pressure from the Nationalists in his government not to appear to kowtow to the Chinese. Nonetheless, as a younger generation of Chinese grow up with only history books to tell them of the war, and Japanese comics and pop stars to woo them, the tension between the two nations may begin to soften regardless of what politicians do or say. One school of thought says that the Americans have been wooing the Japanese as a buttress against the rise of China, especially in relation to Taiwan. If Japan and China end up the best of friends, America may be faced with an entirely different dilemma.

CHAPTER 9   OLYMPIC CHINA

'Building a New Beijing and Welcome the Olympics.'
Banner in Beijing

In March 2007, Beijingers began to learn a new word, mai. Some Beijing newspapers helpfully provided pronunciation guides just to make sure Beijingers knew how to say it. *Mai* means 'haze' and it was the word city officials wanted to use to describe the dirty grey fog that shrouds Beijing, one of the world's most polluted cities, for much of the year. In the past, officials had always referred to the phenomenon euphemistically as wu, which is a rather gentle word meaning 'mist', as if naming it kindly would somehow mitigate its effects and distract from its real cause – smoke belching from Beijing's factories, dust billowing up from its eight thousand construction sites and exhaust fumes blown out by its ever-increasing motor traffic. Admitting that wu was really mai was an indication of just how desperately China wants to make a good impression at the Beijing Olympics in 2008.

Being awarded the Olympics in 2001 was a red letter day for China. When the International Olympic Committee (IOC) announced that Beijing had beaten off the competition from Toronto, Paris, Istanbul and Osaka, the streets of Beijing erupted with Olympic fever. In some ways, for ordinary Beijingers, it was like emerging from the dark into the light. Finally, the grim days were behind them and China had been recognised as a vibrant, great country. Up and down the country, young people especially, swapped texts and blogs saying, 'I love China!!!'

The Party, too, was no doubt feeling in a party mood. Although the IOC does not base its choice on economic respectability, it clearly takes into account the host's ability to fund the event properly. When Tokyo was awarded the Olympics in 1964, it seemed to be in recognition of Japan's amazing economic boom and its final emergence from the dark post-war days. Similarly when Seoul was awarded the games in 1988, it seemed a fitting stamp on South Korea's extraordinary rise to prosperity. So when Beijing got the 2008 games, it was widely seen as China's economic coming-out party – the international seal of approval on China's economic boom.

Beijing dynamo

In some ways, the Beijing Olympics are the biggest (good) thing that has happened to China for a long, long time, and the Party, at least, has thrown itself into the event with

PROFILE: DENG YAPING

Deng Yaping is a legend in China. This tiny woman, just 1.49 metres (4 feet 11 inches) tall, was voted by Chinese people Chinese athlete of the twentieth century in 2003, and quite rightly, for she is one of the greatest table-tennis players of all time. She was born on 5 February 1973 in Zhengzhou in Henan. When she was nine years old she won a provincial junior championship but wasn't allowed to play on the team because she was too short. When she was thirteen, Deng won the national championship, but wasn't allowed to play on the national team because she was too short. But when she was sixteen, coaches finally relented and let her play, and she immediately won the world table-tennis doubles title with Qiao Hong. Two years later, in 1991, she beat North Korean star Li Bun-hui to win the world singles title. The following year at the Barcelona Olympics, she swept all before her to win both the singles and the doubles gold medals. She repeated the feat at the 1996 Olympics. Not surprisingly, she was world number one female table-tennis player from 1990 to 1997. When she retired that year at the age of just 24, she had won more titles than any other player in the history of table tennis. Since then she has played a key role in the Olympic movement, and led the team that won Beijing the 2008 Olympics. No wonder she is a bit of a star in Beijing.

astonishing enthusiasm and energy. Whether ordinary Chinese people feel the same way remains to be seen, but there is no doubting the commitment from the top. The direct budget for the games is US$40 billion – two-and-a-half times London's budget for 2012 – and this is probably just a tiny fraction of the massive amount being spent on the dramatic makeover of Beijing ahead of the games.

Beijing is now going through a transformation that is more radical, if anything, than that which began in Shanghai in the early 1990s. Visitors who last travelled to the city in 1990 would simply not recognise it today. Indeed, even locals find it hard to find their way around, so much has changed and so many familiar landmarks have vanished as the mania of development proceeds. Beijing had none of the worries and problems with existing inhabitants that beset London in finding a suitable site for the Olympic village. To create Beijing's Olympic site, the city simply evicted the occupants of a slum district that was once home to tens of thousands of people, and bulldozed away their old homes. So determined are the planners to give the city a modern facelift that they seem to be moving heaven and earth, and most of Beijing, to do so.

On Tiananmen Square there is a placard that ticks off the days to Olympic opening day, and every day really counts. Beijing set itself the goal of building or renovating 72 sports stadiums and training arenas, carving out 59 new roads and building 3 new bridges – not to mention a new cross-city underground, a new airport, a host of offices for the press and media, new houses and new hotels, and much more besides. Yet Beijing seems to have taken the whole gargantuan task in its stride, bussing in huge armies of construction workers from the countryside to work six-month stints. Observers seeing forty thousand people working on the new airport and seven thousand on the National Stadium have commented that this is the closest you get to seeing what it must have been like when they built the Great Wall of China. A year before the event, the bulk of the work was done, and many of the workers have been shipped back to their villages – leaving the glamorous new Beijing they have built, it is said, for the foreigners and the Beijing elite to enjoy.

Design arena

Beijing is a huge, crowded, dirty city but there is no doubt that the Olympic planners are going all the way to put on a spectacular show. They have hired the West's most prestigious, most innovative architects and given them their head. Architectural journalist Deyan Sudjic sees China using the Olympics 'as the chance to make a defiant and unmistakable statement that the country has taken its place in the world'. World-renowned British architect Norman Foster has been brought in to design Beijing's new international airport – a stunning, super-slick building in the shape of a dragon. Controversial Dutch architect Rem Koolhaas has given Central China TV a new headquarters that has been described as 'a skyscraper tumbling into a somersault', 'a person kneeling' or even 'a doughnut'. Koolhaas was also on the design committee that awarded the design contract for the main stadium to the Swiss partnership of Herzog and de Meuron, who updated London's Tate Modern gallery. Herzog and de Meuron's National Stadium is certainly a startling creation, made from a web of steel columns and beams. It has already been nicknamed 'the bird's nest' by locals. This is an auspicious name, since a bird's nest is a harmonious natural object, and an expensive delicacy on the table. One project, however, has received the mocking nickname 'the egg' – Paul Andreu's generally disliked National Grand Theatre near Tiananmen Square.

BEIJING NATIONAL AQUATICS CENTRE

The new National Stadium built for the 2008 Olympics in Beijing, nicknamed 'the bird's nest', has already attracted a fair amount of attention for its highly original design. But right next door, the Beijing Olympics team have built another Olympics venue that will be, if anything, even more striking: the National Aquatics Centre, designed by Australian design partnership Arup/PTW, the China State Construction and Engineering Corporation and the Shenzhen Design Institute. Already nicknamed the Water Cube, this startlingly original building was inspired by water bubbles, and looks like nothing more than a slice chopped out of the foam on a bubble bath. The walls of the centre have a metal framework of shapes that are based on research about the random shapes of soap bubbles, plant cells, crystals and molecules. Filling in the spaces in between are pillows made of ultra-thin fluorocarbon ETFE (ethylene tetrafluoroethylene) membranes. The membranes are sewn into the structure and then inflated. The idea is that the Water Cube will be the cool, moist *yang* (female) to the National Stadium's fiery *yin* (male), but the ETFE pillow walls, normally azure blue, can change to startling red in moments with a simple lighting change.

Manchurian makeover

Beijing's facelift doesn't stop with the buildings. They are determined to clean up the city to present it in the best possible light to the world. Air pollution is indeed a key issue, as indicated by the adoption of the word *mai*. Beijing has no intention of athletes complaining that they can't perform properly because of the quality of the air. According to the *People's Daily*, Beijing is spending US$3 billion on pollution control ahead of the games in 2007 alone. Not only are they mounting tighter emissions controls on vehicles, but they have moved one of the city's dirtiest factories, a steel plant in the western suburbs, out to an offshore suburb. That so much of this might be about China's image rather than genuine concern with environmental health is indicated by some of the measures the authorities are thought to be taking for the Olympics. The Beijing authorities intend to shut down all polluting factories (but only for the duration of the games) and ban many of the city's cars (again only for the duration of the games). According to Beijing's vice-mayor Ji Lin, 'Car control, that is to temporarily ban some of the cars, is necessary for both traffic administration and air pollution control.'

It is widely believed they will clear the streets of all beggars and vagrants during the games, too, but the authorities have denied reports that they will expel three million migrant workers from the city, round up prostitutes and confine mentally ill people in hospitals. Yet to make sure the streets are clean, even foreigners are now being handed rubbish bags for their litter on arrival, and dozens of people have already been fined for spitting in the street, a common Beijing habit that the authorities are keen to see disappear before the games. Every month on the eleventh is now Queuing Day in Beijing, the day when Chinese people learn how to form orderly queues under the guidance of satin-sashed Queuing Day volunteers, with officials sometimes handing out a rose to the most orderly 'queuer'.

THE ENGLISH MENU

The Beijing authorities are determined not to be embarrassed in any way when the foreigners show up for the games in 2008. So it was with some horror that they realised that the English translations generously provided on signs and menus all over Beijing to help foreigners, as well as providing good advertising, could be hilarious to their targets. So, according to an article by Jim Yardley in the *New York Times*, academics have been enlisted to go around the city spotting mistranslations and providing the correct translation.

They've noticed some real corkers. Tourists to Beijing, for instance, are invited to take a trip to 'Racist Park', a theme park about China's ethnic minorities. And they are tempted on restaurant menus to try the local delicacy crab, spelled with a 'p' not a 'b'. A favourite is pullet, a young hen, apparently translated as a 'sexually inexperienced chicken'. Fortunately, some have already been changed. The Dongda Anus Hospital is now known as the Dongda Proctology Hospital.

There is little doubt that economically the Olympic Games have been good for Beijing. China's economy as a whole is swelling pretty fast at the moment, but Beijing's is swelling faster still. While China's economy is growing by 10 per cent or more a year, Beijing's has grown even faster at over 12 per cent in the run-up to the Olympics. There are those who worry, though, that once the Olympics are gone, the plug on the city's prosperity could be pulled. Two Beijing academics, Liu Qiyun and Wang Junping, argue that because Beijing's spending on the games has been so heavy – half as much as all the previous eight games put together – the typical investment downturn afterwards could be unusually severe, landing the city in a major slump.

Game critics

There are people who criticise the Beijing games for different reasons. Beijing was always a controversial choice for the games because of its human-rights record. Some people even likened it to the awarding of the 1936 Olympics to Berlin under the Nazis. While most wouldn't go that far, there is no doubt that China will be under close scrutiny. Some observers have suggested that awarding the games might put pressure on China to make progress by putting it in the international spotlight. In an article in *Business Week*, Laura D'Andrea Tyson, a former adviser to Bill Clinton, wrote that, 'Paradoxically, hosting the games is likely to be a boon for China's citizenry and a headache for their leaders.' Yet others have said that their successful bid for the Olympics, along with China's growing prosperity, has simply given the country's leaders the confidence to ride roughshod over moral condemnation from abroad. Of particular concern is China's role in Darfur (see pages 126–7), provoking many to call the Beijing games the 'Genocide Olympics', but the fate of Tibet, political prisoners, conditions in China's factories (including child labour) and China's environmental record are all attracting critical attention.

Interestingly, this is creating something of a public relations nightmare for the global corporations sponsoring the Olympics such as Adidas, Coca-Cola, General Electric, McDonald's and Kodak. If these companies completely ignore activists' criticisms, they might turn off consumers at home. Yet if they criticise the Chinese, they could jeopardise their future in this hugely lucrative market. In the past, the Chinese authorities have been quick to drop licences or operating agreements with foreign corporations to which they take a dislike. But at home companies such as Coca-Cola and McDonald's are facing some high-profile critics. Actress Mia Farrow, chair of a group called Dream for Darfur, is reported to have written in an email, 'The Olympics will be forever tarnished unless China uses its influence to get Khartoum to act [on Darfur]; the brands of the sponsors will be tarnished by association.' PR for the corporations tries to steer a safe line by saying that they have no power to influence sovereign governments, and by emphasising their other humanitarian projects, but the issues are certain to be raised.

TORCH MARCH

To get the 2008 games started, Beijing is planning the longest ever Olympic torch relay. The flame will start as usual at Olympia in Greece, on 25 March 2008, and then will travel 137,000 kilometres (85,000 miles) across five continents before it finally arrives in the National Stadium in Beijing to commence the games. En route it will travel right along the old Silk Road through cities such as Samarkand and Tashkent in Uzbekistan to symbolise how far back the links go between China and the rest of the world. The relay is called the Journey of Harmony, but the planning has not been completely harmonious. One proposed stop en route is at Taipei in Taiwan, but the Taiwanese government is not happy with this, saying that since Taiwan is not part of China, the Chinese cannot simply decide unilaterally to take the route through Taiwan. Another contentious part of the plan is to carry the flame to the top of Mount

Qomolangma (Everest). It is not so much the carrying of the torch up the mountain that upsets environmentalists and Tibetan rights campaigners but the 108-kilometre (67-mile) tarmacked highway the Chinese are building through the fragile Himalayan environment all the way to Everest Base Camp. During the torch relay, the Everest highway will carry all the support and media. Afterwards, though, the road will become a major way in for tourists and climbers who want to reach the mountain the easy way.

Whatever the outcome of the Olympics, there is no doubt whatsoever that it will put the new China on the map. Billions of people around the world will see for the first time the startling changes that China has gone through, they will see on their TV screens the amazing modern architecture of China's cities and they will see Chinese people out in the streets enjoying themselves wearing as wide a range of fashions as anyone in the West. No one will ever again be able to think of Chinese people as downtrodden and wearing the drab pajamas of the Mao era.

CHAPTER 10   YOUNG CHINA

'Maybe in the past, everyone was obedient and listened to the old grannies who lectured on who you could have sex with and in what position. But we don't have time to listen. We're too busy having sex.'

Young blogger Li, quoted in
***Time* magazine, December 2005**

Towards the end of the 1990s, the Chinese media began to pick up on a new phenomenon. A few young Chinese people in cities such as Shanghai were starting to look and behave very strangely. In the West, people perhaps wouldn't give them a second look. With their dark clothes, heavy make-up and dyed mops of hair, these young urbanites resembled nothing more than toned-down Goths. With their taste for heavy smoking and gloomy rock music à la Kurt Cobain or Chinese punk bands like Brain Failure, they were in some ways a mélange of western youth cultures from punk to Generation X, with just a little Chinese twist. The West is now used to these shifts of youthful rebellion, but for the Chinese it was all something of a shock.

The media dubbed these 20-something Bohemians the 'Weiku generation'. Weiku combined the Chinese words *wei* and *ku* meaning 'great' and 'extreme', but it was also a witty play on the American youth phrase 'way cool'. The word was already a little passé among the Chinese youngsters who used it but the label stuck. The Weiku generation were born in the 1970s, after the Cultural Revolution, and the China they grew up in was not the China of Mao and the hardline Communists. As the Weikus went through their childhood, China was undergoing the first of the reforms that began to open it up to the rest of the world. By the time they were in their teens, western influences were beginning to seep through, and young Chinese were beginning to reject some of the values of their parents.

Web take-off

Interestingly, many of the Chinese who were just a decade older than the Weikus – the 30-somethings of the 1990s – had left China to study in America, before the reforms had really begun to kick in. These emigrés came back eager to introduce the wonders of the Internet to China's young, and created China's own dot.com bubble in 1999–2000. Often capitalised by American funding, they launched a host of new portals and search engines to fire China's 'Generation Yellow', as they called it, into the Internet age. Sites such as E-Tang, Sohu.com, Sina.com and Netease gave the infant Chinese Web a host of new start-ups, and American business, expecting great things from them, poured in massive funding.

There was no doubt that this kick-started the Chinese Web into life, but the Chinese dot.com entrepreneurs, returning bright-eyed from America, were unaware just how much China had changed in their absence. Believing they were both tuned in with the latest trends in the western world, and their Chinese culture as well, they didn't realise how little they had in common with their compatriots just a decade or so younger. These 1960s children were often idealistic and optimistic – in complete contrast to the Weiku, who are sometimes referred to as the *kuadiao yi dai*, the 'collapsed generation' for their cynicism and self-obsession.

FANTASY LAND

Things Japanese are very cool with young people in China, despite the enmity in the country towards Japan as a country, and Japanese comics and animation attract ardent fans. One of the big crazes in China in the last few years has been the role-playing game Cosplay, which also came from Japan. In Cosplay, teenagers dress up and act out stories involving their favourite cartoon or computer game. For some young people, Cosplay has become more a way of life than just a game, but there is no doubting its wide appeal among the young. In a world that's changing fast, and lacking true guidance, these fantasy games are a welcome escape. The whole idea of Cosplay goes hand in hand with the growing need of young Chinese to make a mark. In the days when China was based on a collective spirit, or in imperial times, it was easy to find your place in life, but now young Chinese feel much more on their own – and on their own in a country of a over a billion people. No wonder, then, that many Chinese kids say their dream is to *zuo xiu* (make a show of themselves) and build up their coterie of *fen-si* – literally, *fen-si* means 'rice noodles', but it is a typical young Chinese pun on the English word 'fans'. Cosplay fulfils this idea with the minimum pain, and events can be massive, with tens of thousands of outrageously dressed teenagers ready to perform or just join in the fun.

The result was that these new websites missed their target market almost entirely. They were portal sites – that is, sites that merely act as entry points – and had very little content, and the sites they led to were far too broad and bland for the teens and 20-somethings likely to be connected to the Internet. Taiwanese rapper Zhang Zhenyu said it all about attitudes to the American returnees among the Weikus with his track 'Bullshit' in which he tells them, 'You say you've got an American degree; I say you're just farting.' Very quickly, the big Chinese websites began to struggle.

The communications revolution

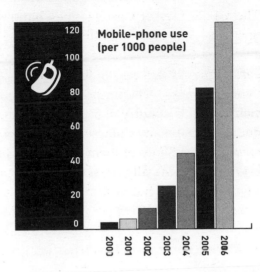

Mobile-phone use
(per 1000 people)

120
100
80
60
40
20
0

2000 2001 2002 2003 2004 2005 2006

The alternative Web

The Weiku generation, though, was the first of the young Chinese to be tech-savvy. So instead of using the flagship portal sites, they began to develop their own special-interest sites – sometimes foreign sites in translation, sometimes home-grown sites. These niche sites focused on specific areas such as graphics, edgy literature or music, like Menkou.com. It was all very underground and alternative, and although rarely politically challenging, the Internet phenomenon began to spread rapidly among China's young.

It would be hard to overestimate the impact of the Internet on Chinese youth. The bare statistics about the rise of the Internet in China are impressive – a few thousand users in 1994,

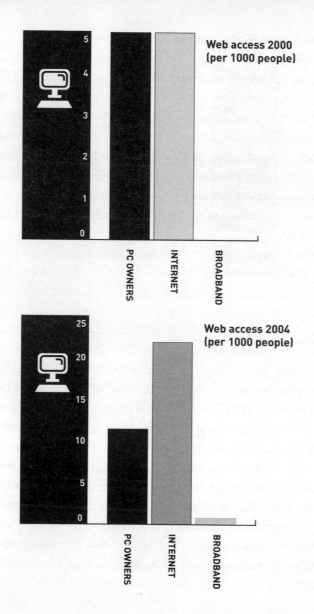

Web access 2000
(per 1000 people)

PC OWNERS
INTERNET
BROADBAND

Web access 2004
(per 1000 people)

PC OWNERS
INTERNET
BROADBAND

4 million in 1999, 21 million in 2001 and 137 million in 2006. But these figures disguise the real impact on the young, especially the urban young, because although not every Chinese youth has their own connection, nearly all can get access, either at school or through Internet cafés. More than 70 per cent of all Chinese children between 7 and 15 have used the Internet at least once, and in towns more than 87 per cent have. Actually, more than half of town-dwelling children live in homes with an Internet connection, and of course it is the tech-savvy young rather than their parents who make the most of it.

Internet use, though, has moved on a long way in just a short time since the Weiku generation, who China's current youngsters already see as being a little out of touch. In the Weiku days, the Internet was very much a message board for a narrow alternative culture. Now it has moved into the mainstream, and is an integral part of life for the urban young. We are familiar in the West with the sheer amount of time young people devote to the Internet, but in Chinese cities it has become, if anything, more extreme. The urban young, to an unprecedented degree, are left to themselves. Because of China's one-child policy, which was far more rigidly enforced in the cities, very few urban children have siblings, and the increasing pressures on income mean that both parents often have to work. Left to their own devices, the often lonely Chinese young find the Internet a tremendous resource, both for making contacts through chat rooms and following up interests. (For the young, it is increasingly friends who matter, not family.)

YOUNG CHINESE STARS

The rapid growth of the media among young Chinese has spawned a host of stars who, if they are yet little known in the rest of the world, are very big in China. There are movie and pop stars such as Hong Kong-based Edison Chen, Cecilia Chung and Nic Tse, whose song 'Jade Butterfly' was a huge hit. There are controversial Web writers such as Han Han. There are basketball stars such as the 2.3 metre (7-foot 6-inch) giant Yao Ming who now plays for the Houston Rockets in the US NBA (National Basketball Association), and the Athens Olympics hurdle hero Liu Xiang. The biggest star, however, is the unlikely Taiwanese pop star Jay Chou, listed by British Chatham House think tank in 2007 as one of the 50 most influential people in China. Called *Yu tsun* ('stupid') by his teachers at school, and ugly by his classmates, Jay Chou has defied the odds by writing soulful songs that seem to capture the heart of his adoring female fans. Panasonic has a picture of Jay Chou stamped on its mobile phones, and *Time* magazine ran a major feature on him in 2003.

The knowledge gap

Interestingly, the Internet has helped open up a tremendous knowledge gap between the young and adults. As Sun Yun Xiao of the China Youth and Children Research Center says, 'The Internet has given Chinese children wings.' The Internet gives the young a degree of contact with and knowledge of the outside world that is barely imaginable to their parents. They can follow the progress of the Miami Heat baseball team in the US. They can listen in to the latest R'n'B in New York. Or join chat rooms with teens all over the world. That their interests are no less superficial than teens the world over may not seem very revolutionary, but that very similarity is perhaps the point. It may be this cultural shift among young people that forces China to become more open in a way that no amount of politically charged comment ever can.

The older generation is already feeling the chill of this wind of change. At school, teachers are beginning to feel threatened not just by the knowledge that children have acquired beyond their control, but also by their more challenging attitude. In the old days, Chinese children would accept what the teacher said without question, and respect for elders was an age-old hallmark of Chinese society. Now children are not just more willing to ask why, but can actually be dismissive when they find their teachers are ill-informed and some teachers are finding this very unnerving.

The shock of the young

Parents, if anything, are feeling even more worried. The world around them is changing at a frightening pace – yet their children take it all in their stride in a way that is even more undermining. All too many parents have to rely on their children to tell them what to buy when they go shopping in the new malls, tagging along meekly as their precocious youngsters point out the best brands. A survey showed that in family debates in China, children talked for more than half the time, parents for about a third and grandparents sat mostly in silence – a complete reversal of the traditional pattern.

Yet the generation gap opening up is far more profound than simply shopping advice and dinner-table chats. With their exposure to the outside world, not just on the Internet, but increasingly on TV, too, Chinese teenagers are often much less hung-up about the enmities that drove their parents. Japan and Taiwan are top on China's blacklist, even now, but that's no obstacle to Chinese youngsters who see much of the coolest stuff coming out of Japan and Taiwan. Many Japanese bands, comics and animations are huge with Chinese teenagers; and Taiwanese music and TV is so popular in China that many young Chinese from Beijing and Shanghai are even beginning to speak with the softer, more casual accent of Taiwan, rather than the clipped formality of northern Mandarin – much to their parents' irritation.

WAY OUT IN TIBET

Like every western country, China has its share of young dreamers chasing an alternative lifestyle. For the Weiku generation, Tibet was the coolest place on earth. It all began in the mid-1990s when singer Zheng Jun rode his motorbike across the high Tibetan plateau in his video for the hit song 'Hui Dao Lasa' ('Back to Lhasa'). At that time, Tibet was a tourist destination for just a few tens of thousands, mostly

foreigners. But after Zheng Jun's song, travellers returning from Tibet were like celebrities, the coolest guys in
town and the ones with the explorer spirit. Before long,
more and more young Chinese people were going off
backpacking in Tibet to demonstrate their spirit of adventure and independence, and by 2004 well over a million
were heading west into the mountains each year. The new
road to Everest (see pages 185–6) is expected to boost the
figures to nearly two million. But it is not just travelling
to Tibet that has taken off. Now the Weikus have come of
age and have cash to spare, they are buying into all things
Tibetan. Tibetan jewellery, clothing and even furniture are
now being sold in earthy, organic Tibetan-style shops in the
most flashy malls in Beijing, such as Wangfujing. There are
now even Tibetan-style restaurants serving such delights
as yak-butter tea. Tibetan folk music and Tibetan-inspired
music has become the soothing, inspirational background
to many a young urban Chinese designer lifestyle, with
tracks like Dadawa's 'Sister Drum' and 'Voices from the
Sky' achieving huge success.

The F4 virus

In 2002, Chinese TV stations, keen to attract younger viewers,
began screening a Taiwanese drama series inspired by a Japanese cartoon. Called *Meteor Garden*, it told the story of four
arrogant, rich, outrageously good-looking, baseball–playing,
rock-singing playboy students and the poor girl who refused
to be impressed by their careless ways. Chinese teenagers

loved it, and the series' four young stars, known together as F4, became heart-throbs with teenage girls across the country. As the show gained more attention, so parents and media alike began to complain about the show: its bullying and gangs, its disrespect towards teachers and its emphasis on romance.

As newspapers led the way with headlines like 'Is F4 a virus?', the Chinese broadcasting authorities decided to pull the plug on the show – which only went to show how out of touch they were with the changes that were going on. Instantly, pirate DVDs of *Meteor Garden* began to sell in millions, Internet sites began to exchange info and gossip, and magazines carried countless articles about the F4 boys. Then finally F4 released a pop album, which became an instant best-seller. F4 mania gripped the country – until the next big thing, of course.

THE VOICE OF THE YOUNG

The biggest hit of 2005 with young viewers was a series called *Supergirl*. *Supergirl* was the Chinese equivalent of *Pop Idol*. *Supergirl* drew staggering audiences of over a hundred million. Such was the success of the show that it has spawned a host of imitators such as *My Hero* and *My Show*. Chinese media are now falling over themselves to include 'young' content, from reality shows to Taiwanese- and Japanese-style soaps. Even the state TV channels now realise they have to start appealing to the young if they are not to be left behind. But what was especially interesting about *Supergirl* was its interaction with the audience.

First of all, the winner of the show was 21-year-old Li Yuchun. Li Yuchun was not a conventional Chinese beauty singing a 'safe' song, but a lanky, spiky-haired tomboy who sang the slightly alternative song 'Zombies' by the Irish group the Cranberries. Li Yuchun became an unlikely national celebrity, along with equally unconventional runner-up Zhou Bichang, and the pair went on to appear in numerous ads and TV shows together. The Post Office even issued Li Yuchun stamps.

The second interesting aspect of *Supergirl* audience interaction was that tens of millions of young Chinese voted for Yuchun via text messages. Now almost every youth show has this element of audience participation and voting. This is not surprising for a generation that expects the kind of involvement you get on the Internet, but many people have begun to wonder how long a generation which is getting used to expressing its opinion and voting on 'trivial' matters can be denied a vote on more serious political matters. Most youngsters say they are not that interested in politics and simply want to get on with their lives, but almost all of them are concerned about the environment if not the political issues that worried their parents.

Teenage romance

In the West, the idea of teenage girls going delirious over a boy band is hardly new, but for Chinese parents the whole F4 episode was all rather shocking. The sexual revolution was disturbing in the West even though it stretched over almost a century, but in China it has been compressed into a single decade. It is not just that sex before marriage is something the older generation of Chinese could not even imagine – the concept of even having a boyfriend or girlfriend was alien. Chinese parents find the whole idea that their young sons or daughters might have even a platonic relationship unacceptable. Among the young, however, attitudes are changing, and countless young Chinese boys and girls are having romances hidden from their parents, greatly aided by mobile phones, which give a degree of privacy unknown to their parents when they were young.

Much to the concern of the older generation, many Chinese teenagers, especially girls, are also being swept away on a tide of romance. Adolescent girls lap up teenage romance novels in gigantic numbers, and Valentine's Day, called Lovers' Day in China, has become a hugely popular event among the young. It's all been rather shocking for many older Chinese, but they are now having to get used to the idea of young lovers kissing and holding hands in public, something that would have been unimaginable in the collectivist days of their own youth.

The coming of sex

Until recently, romance was about as far as most Chinese youngsters went. Back in 1989, barely 15 per cent of Beijingers had sex before marriage. By 2004, however, 60–70 per cent had. And they were not just having sex before marriage;

they were having it younger, too. In 2000, a survey of young Chinese boys and girls showed that 43 per cent still managed to hang on to their virginity until they were at least 22, and only 6 per cent lost it before the age of 19. By 2005, there was a dramatic shift as half of all teenagers admitted they had sex before they were 17 – and many were at it much, much earlier. Even the Weiku generation was on average 24 when they first had sex, so the change has been quite startling.

Now the cat's out of the bag, as it were, many young Chinese are throwing themselves vigorously into sex, maybe eager to find out what they have been missing. A few years ago there was a whole spate of sexual confessions by girls turned into best-selling novels or much-visited websites. First up were Zhou Weihui's salacious *Shanghai Baby* and Mian Mian's *Candy*. Then came Chun Sue's *Beijing Doll*, which sold 100,000 copies in China within a few weeks of its publication in May 2002. Chun Sue was only 17 at the time, and it told the explicit semi-autobiographical story of a string of disappointing sexual encounters starting at the age of just 14. *Beijing Doll* gave rise to a cult following among a group of disaffected Chinese youth who identified with Sue's bleak outlook and fascination with sex and western rock music. Then in 2003 came Muzi Mei's online diary of her sexual encounters, which included a podcast complete with her enthusiastic moans during one session, which scored so many website hits that the system crashed. The Chinese authorities banned all of these, of course, but to little effect since copies of the books were widely circulated on the black market and the tech-savvy youngsters found their way to material on other sites.

In 2002, the arrest of a group of high-school girls in Kunming attracted a lot of bewildered attention. The girls were accused of running a prostitution ring with fifty of their classmates, some as young as 13. The girls were neither coerced into it, nor driven by poverty or even depression. It seems they were just curious, and flattered by male attention and gifts. It was a shocking event, but perhaps just the most extreme reaction to the long years of repression now being released.

LEARNING THE CHINESE WAY

The Chinese have always put enormous store on the value of education. From the time of Confucius, it was clear that you had to study hard to get on in life. In the last few decades, though, it has become something of an obsession. With the old jobs and housing for life system swept away by the reforms, parents and children alike are certain that the only way to ensure a foot on the ladder in the future is with the best education.

Even before they go to school, Chinese children are crammed with lessons in everything from English to calligraphy, and once they start school the pace of work would scare a western child to death. Even ordinary schools demand several hours of homework each night from children virtually from the moment they begin school aged 6. Some of the top 'pressure' schools that are becoming ever more popular among the well-to-do push young children even harder.

As they get older, the pace accelerates, reaching a peak in the final three years of high school. These are the years in which students prepare for the dreaded *gaokao*, the higher-education exam that every student who wants to go to university must sit. Such is the importance of these three-day exams, and the terror they inspire, that parents wait outside the school like trainers in the Tour de France, ready to ply their sons and daughters with energy-giving snacks whenever they emerge from the examination hall for a break.

The pressure reached breaking point in the late 1990s, when five million students sat the *gaokao* to secure just one-and-a-half million university places. The Chinese government suddenly woke up to the problem and has begun a massive university expansion programme that has already boosted the number of university places to four million. It's an astonishing achievement, but has only eased the pressure a little since demand for places in higher education has shot up dramatically – and four million is just a tiny percentage of Chinese children of university age.

To cater for the demand both at university level and for schools that give children a push up the ladder, there has been an explosion of private schools and colleges in the last few years, and people are prepared to pay fortunes to get their child a place. Interestingly, some of these private colleges have been adding a new dimension to Chinese education. There has been a feeling that the rigid rote-learning that is the norm in Chinese schools is so at odds with the increasingly questioning minds of young Chinese that it is demotivating. It may be, too, that this fact-cramming approach was fine in the past, but will not produce the creativity many believe China will need if it is to sustain its economic progress. In his book *Getting Rich First*, Duncan Hewitt describes the privately run Jianqiao Insitute outside Shanghai, where the teaching encourages a more questioning, creative attitude from students, along with the active engagement of students with businesses and community projects. It may be that this kind of approach will catch on.

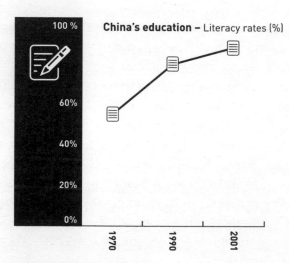

China's education – Literacy rates (%)

Source: China Statistical Yearbook, 2005

Getting left behind?

Although the Kunming schoolgirl vice ring was the most extraordinary case, it is clear that a wide generation gap has opened up between young Chinese and their elders, and the changes are happening fast. The Weiku generation has already been displaced by the '1980s generation' which, in turn, is giving way to the '1990s generation', the children who have known nothing but life post the 1991 reforms.

It is the gap between the 1990s generation and their parents that is perhaps most marked. The parents of these children were children themselves during the Cultural Revolution. As children they were caught up in the worst excesses of the Revolution and the Red Guard movement – and when it was over they were sent away from home to work on collectives, and were deprived of any further education. This whole generation is not simply ill-informed about the world, but carries a weight of sadness and expectation for their own children that the children cannot possibly live up to.

Unfortunately, this weight of expectation is often focused on a single child, for members of the 1990s generation are products of China's one-child policy at its peak. The parents have to pin all their hopes and dreams on just a single child. No wonder some of these children have turned rebellious and sullen, unable to share the burden of their parents' expectations. The pressure on them to do well is enormous, and many of them are given a heavy dose of piano lessons, calligraphy and foreign-language study even before they arrive at primary school.

On the other hand, these single children, especially the much wanted boys, are very likely to be pampered by their parents – and not just their parents, but both sets of grandparents, too, who tend to look after the child now urban parents spend more time out working. It's hardly surprising that these children are often thought to be spoiled and have been dubbed 'little emperors' for the way they rule over the whole family roost. In some ways, the Internet and other modern media have made them hugely more knowledgeable than their parents and grandparents, but all the pampering means they often have no idea how to look after themselves in even a basic way.

The 'me' generation

Sometimes, the young Chinese of today are characterised as the 'me' generation. They are often criticised for being self-obsessed and self-centred, and totally focused on consumer rewards and self-gratification. It's certainly true that many believe their own needs come first. In the BBC World Service series *Young in China*, a young musician, Long Kuan, says: 'What's important to me is myself. I think the first responsibility I have is to myself. And then you think about other people. You can do whatever you want, as long as it doesn't hurt any other people.'

This concentration on personal needs and a *laissez-faire* attitude to others at first seems totally at odds with the collective and very rigid mindset of the parents of these young Chinese. It seems demanding and selfish compared to the community spirit of the older generation. But in some senses, it may be that they are the first generation since the Communist Revolution that has had to stand on its own feet. In their parents' time, people were, in some ways at least, cared for from cradle to grave, given at least basic work, food and housing for life. But in the 1990s, the 'iron rice bowl' of support was rudely snatched away. Today's young are growing up in a world where they alone are responsible for their housing, food, healthcare and work, and perhaps they are aware they have to have basic survival skills their parents never needed.

ALIASES

INFO

Perhaps anxious not to get lost with an ordinary Chinese name among the hundreds of millions of their contemporaries, all the coolest kids on the Chinese block give themselves soubriquets. Chinese youngsters love English names that have a punning effect in Chinese, or vice versa. But Japanese names are popular, too, often inspired by favourite cartoon characters.

There is no doubt that some of the young are frightened by the world that has opened up to them. Others feel trapped by the restrictions of the authoritarian world that still tries to mould their thoughts and their lives. Not surprisingly, some have gone off the rails, with depression or drugs. Yet the vast majority of China's young seem to be bursting with energy, excited by the new possibilities that are coming into their lives and determined to make the most of them. The future won't be easy, and Chinese society is becoming more and more divided between the haves and the have-nots, but for those who fall on the right side, the huge ambition and drive of young people could change China for good.

CHAPTER 11   WHITHER CHINA?

'When I let go of who I am, I become what I might be.'
Lao Tzu, Taoist philosopher, (6th century BCE)

China is a hugely complex country, and has baffled and fooled many Western observers time and time again, so it would be a mistake to try and make any predictions for the future, or even make too much of summing up where it is now. There are, however, some things which are clear. China appears to be changing, and changing fast.

China's cities are swelling at a fantastic rate and being transformed by a construction boom that is throwing up the kind of skyscrapers and shopping malls that would make most Western cities look tired. There is a new generation of young Chinese people growing up in these cities whose education comes from neither the teachings of Confucius nor Mao's *Little Red Book*, but the Internet and TV. There are people of all generations in these cities who are acquiring wealth their ancestors barely dreamed of, and using it to pay for the full range of consumer goods, from DVD players to Gucci bags. Many ordinary Chinese people are even beginning to see the world as they travel abroad on holidays. At the same time hundreds of millions of people in the countryside have been freed from the kind of grinding poverty that once afflicted most of China's peasants. They too are becoming familiar with the consumer comforts most of us in the West take for granted, and most of them are more literate and in better health than people living in other countries that have been such a short time on the road to development.

All of this is something the Chinese people and their leaders can be immensely proud of. It is an astonishing achievement, and the energy and vibrancy of many Chinese cities shows they know it and know they can go further. There is no doubt many Chinese people feel that at last their time has come, and they will take their place on the world stage, leading it rather than simply following.

The people's republic?

On the other hand, none of this seems to have opened the way to democracy, nor offered the kind of freedom of expression that most Westerners believe is essential for a healthy society. The media is still heavily monitored, the Internet is censored, and access to much Western news is still filtered by a dedicated army of information police. Moreover, dissenters certainly live in fear of the machinery of state repression. Even though there have not recently been events as traumatic as Tiananmen Square, protesters are frequently treated with brutality if things get a little out of hand.

There certainly have been protests, and the number of protests has been rising. Yet these protests have not been about democracy but about local issues such as environmental damage and land seizures. Every day, there are hundreds of small protests like these. None involve more than a few thousand people, but they are bitter enough, and it is quite common for a few protesters to be killed by the police as they try to keep them under control. It is hard to tell whether this rising tide of protest is purely about local grievances, as most pundits say, or whether it is something deeper that can only find an outlet in these smaller issues – and may build up into a far more fundamental drive for change that eventually becomes irresistible.

It is no accident that most of these protests are in the countryside where people have benefited least from the wealth that has poured into the country in the last fifteen years. There are hundreds of millions of people in the Chinese countryside for whom life is still very hard indeed, and many of them face injustices that are difficult to imagine from greedy officials and rapacious developers. If anyone has any reason in China to rebel against the system, it is these people. Although there are plenty of poor, downtrodden people in the cities, most can see lives improving around them, while many others are now either too busy trying to earn a living, or too comfortable, to worry quite so much about politics.

Leading the way?

People may wonder why the Communist Party is so afraid of democratic freedoms if, as they say, the people are so contented with the way things are going and the prosperity they are bringing the country. Surely that would be the icing on the cake and the final successful chapter in the People's Revolution? There are, of course, all kinds of ideological reasons why not. Yet perhaps there are other, more pragmatic reasons, too. Now the Party has been in power for so long, there are far too many vested interests in preserving its status. Too many officials have got used to power and the privileges it brings to give it up, and China is such a vast country that even if the central leadership wish to make changes there is no guarantee that local leaders may not try to thwart their aims. Many Chinese leaders feel a move to democracy would open a can of worms and lead to a dog-eat-dog society that exploits the weak rather than open the way to a stable, free society.

With President Hu and premier Wen, China seems to have two leaders who are aware of the problems of a divided society. They have introduced measures to shift some of the benefits of China's wealth towards the poor, to tackle environmental problems and create a more obviously rational, open form of government. It may be an illusion, but they seem highly unlikely to sanction the kind of extreme repression seen in Tiananmen Square. In some ways, they give the impression that China is in safe, reasonable, moderate hands for the first time in the history of the People's Republic. Although they might deny it, the vision of the Harmonious Society they are

working towards seems not so very different from the socialist vision of the old British Labour Party with nationalised
industries and a blanket of welfare support for the less well-
off. The difference is that they are backed up by an entrenched
machine of state repression and the world's largest standing
army.

China steps out

During the Mao years, China kept most of its huge problems
to itself. After the end of the Korean war, Chinese military
might was seen little abroad, and China's trading interaction
with the rest of the world was almost non-existent. Indeed,
so little was known about China that Western students in the
1960s could be seduced by the charm of Mao's *Little Red Book*,
knowing nothing of the true terror of the Cultural Revolution.
Now, however, China is beginning to interact with the world
in a pretty dramatic way. Politically, it seems to be trying to
keep itself to itself. Hu and Wen seem to have done wonders
in creating at least an image of a China that means no harm
and will rise peacefully. Some people are still concerned that
issues such as Taiwan could be flashpoints that will make the
sleeping dragon wake and breathe fire. Yet this seems unlikely
at the moment.

Of more concern, perhaps, is the impact of China's growing economy on the rest of the world. On the one side is the
growing concern in the Western world, and in the USA in particular, that China's swelling industries are robbing people of
their jobs and making it impossible for their home industries

to survive. In July 2007, a war of words seemed to be brewing between China and the USA over the quality of Chinese products, but it is quite possible that the attacks on the quality of Chinese toothpaste and the like are symptomatic of growing hostility in America to China and her trading might.

In December 2007, the US Treasury Secretary noted that China was making some progress in addressing American concerns. But by February 2008, China was facing a raft of World Trade Organization actions over things such as import tariffs on auto parts and its record on protecting Intellectual Property Rights – though some commentators feel that as China generates more and more of its own technological advances, it will naturally toughen up its stance without outside pressure. When official figures revealed that China's trade surplus for January 2008 had actually jumped nearly 20 per cent over the previous January to over $22 billion, the Chinese began to face renewed criticism from the EU and US, who believe China undervalues the Yuan to make its exports artificially cheap.

Another side is China's growing demand for resources. China seems anxious to avoid directly competing with the Western world for resources such as oil, but this has led it to establish links with some unpleasant regimes, such as Mugabe's Zimbabwe and Sudan, much to the annoyance and concern of many Western governments.

Interestingly, though, the Chinese leadership seems to be acknowledging these issues, and looking for a way to deal with them. In some ways, China seems to have reached a degree of political stability under Hu and Wen that will allow the country's prosperity to both continue to grow and spread wider amongst the Chinese population. It may be that the biggest obstacle in its path is not political but environmental – not simply because China already has as big a range of environmental problems as any country in the world, but mainly because China's continued growth will strain the world's resources to breaking point.

In 2008, the Beijing Olympics will allow the world to see into China as never before, and see some of the changes that have happened in that city in particular. Whether the real China becomes any clearer remains to be seen.

BACKGROUND

History

One of the astonishing things about China's civilisation is just how durable it has proved to be. It is undoubtedly ancient – older than Islam, older than Christianity, older than Buddhism, older even than Hinduism, the world's oldest religion. Indeed the first Chinese emperors came to power centuries before the first Roman emperors and, while Rome came and went, the Chinese emperors ruled on and on, until they were finally deposed by their own people less than a century ago. Indeed, it was only with that revolution that the true age of Chinese civilisation has finally begun to be revealed.

While the empire survived, almost the only knowledge about China's ancient past came from imperial histories – written thousands of years ago, but already full of myths and half-remembered truths. The picture of China's origins as painted by these historians was of a civilisation that somehow miraculously appeared almost fully formed some time in the distant past without going through the stages of gradual development, such as a Stone Age, that other cultures did. Only with the revolution did archaeologists and palaeontologists begin to look for hard evidence in the ground and make some key discoveries, such as the prehistoric settlement at Banpo in Shaanxi, which began to reveal the truth. Indeed only in the last thirty years have China's archaeologists made many of the finds that are finally revealing just how China emerged in the distant past.

Prehistoric China
2 million years ago–2000 BCE

It is now clear that China was inhabited far back into the dawn of prehistory. In 1995, bones of hominids were found in China and dated to 1.9 million years ago – much earlier than anyone had thought likely. Then, in 2004, 1.66-million-year-old stone tools were found at Majuangou in northern China. Most palaeontologists now have little doubt that *Homo erectus*, the first hominid to walk out of Africa, reached China earlier than anyone had once thought likely.

After *Homo erectus* came other hominids, such as the famous Beijing man *Sinanthropus pekinensis*, whose half-million-year-old bones were found in a cave near Beijing in 1923, and Lantian man *Sinanthropus lantianensis*, whose six-hundred-thousand-year-old bones were found in Shaanxi in

1923. Other finds suggest that modern humans, *Homo sapiens*, were in China pretty much as early as anywhere in the world – at least eighty thousand years ago, and maybe much, much earlier. It's not known yet when the distinctively featured Chinese race first appeared, but it may be some twenty thousand years ago.

It was once thought that our hunting and gathering ancestors first turned to farming in the Middle East, about ten thousand years ago and the idea only slowly spread east to south-east Asia, over thousands of years. But as more and more archaeological evidence is unearthed, it is becoming clear not only that farming developed independently, and roughly simultaneously, in China – but that it developed in three or more separate regions in China independently, too, and in slightly different ways. Each of these regions had its own distinctive culture.

The first evidence for one of these cultures was found at Yangshao in Henan province in the 1920s, and so is called the Yangshao culture. The Yangshao grew tough, hardy millet on the wind-blown loess soils in Shaanxi, along the Wi River and Yellow River. They also made distinctive painted pottery and stone farm tools, and reared pigs and dogs for food. The Longshan culture lived further south on the Yangtze and Huai valleys, and were growing rice in paddies some ten thousand years ago, as well as rearing dogs, pigs and water-buffalo. The south-eastern culture lived along the south and east coastal plains at least eleven thousand years ago and grew tubers such as taro and yam.

Which, if any, of these cultures was the original Chinese

culture continues to be a source of considerable contention among Chinese historians. One of the problems is that Longshan sites of later date are found in Yanshao regions, and vice versa. The truth is probably that there was considerable intermixing, and each culture contributed something to the development of what we call Chinese civilisation. However, in 1987, a remarkable archaeological find was made in Puyang, 500 kilometres (300 miles) south of Beijing on the banks of the Yellow River. The find was the burial site of a Yangshao tribal chieftain of the Yangshao, but it was no ordinary burial site. Either side of the chief's skeleton, there were 2-metre-long (3½ feet) designs made out of clam shells – one of a tiger, and one of a dragon. The find dates to 6,460 years ago, showing that the dragon and the tiger have been important emblems in Chinese culture for more than six millennia. So central to Chinese culture is the dragon that Puyang is making a big thing of being the site of 'the First Dragon of China', and in June 2007 announced plans for a massive dragon theme park.

Chinese Bronze Age
2000–1046 BCE

The ancient Chinese, though, knew nothing of their Stone Age forebears, whose existence has only been revealed by archaeology. Historians of ancient times, such as Sima, who wrote his famous history of China called *Shiji* about 100 BCE, based their stories of China's origins on legends such as that of Shen Nong who is supposed to have invented herbal medicine, the Yellow Emperor who is credited with developing all the essential features of civilisation – farming, the family, the calendar, silk, boats, carts and archery – and Yu the Great who controlled China's watercourses. Yu the Great was also said to have begun the first of three ancient dynasties of rulers – the Xia, the Shang and the Zhou.

A century ago, many experts thought that most of these histories were mostly myth. But archaeological findings have begun to show that certainly the Zhou and the Shang and maybe even the Xia dynasties actually existed. If the Xia prove to be a real dynasty, then it is likely they first came to power in Shanxi or Henan about 2100–2000 BCE. By this time, as archaeology shows, culture in northern China was becoming much more settled and structured. Villages were developing into walled towns, and society was differentiating into classes – rulers, farmers, merchants, artisans and so on. Then the Chinese discovered how to make bronze, and entered their Bronze Age. Some historians think that the idea of bronze came from the West, but the Chinese shaped bronze in such a distinctive way, using elaborate clay moulds, rather than the hammer and the anvil, that it is quite possible that bronze making developed independently here, too.

Whatever the truth, by the time the Shang came to power about 1600–1500 BCE, the Chinese had developed tremendous skill in making the gigantic bronze urns that are such a distinctive feature of the archaeological finds from this period. The biggest of these was found at Anyang, near the Yellow River in Henan, the site that showed the Shang really existed. Anyang was the Shang capital, and it is not only the signs of a giant bronze foundry here that testifies to their power but also the scale of the royal tombs. Besides chariots, weapons and bronzes, these tombs also contain the remains of hundreds of bodies – slaves and soldiers sacrificed in honour of the dead king. Another Shang city, Zhengzhou, was built with a rampart 9 metres (30 feet) high and 36 metres (120 feet) wide that is thought to have taken ten thousand men eighteen years to build.

The most telling of all the Shang archaeological finds, though, has been the 'dragon bones'. These bones began turning up in the late nineteenth century in traditional medicine shops. They were being sold as magic cures for disease because they were covered in mysterious symbols. Thousands of these bones were found when Anyang was being excavated in the 1920s, and historians began the work of deciphering the symbols. After a lot of work, scholars realised that these symbols were actually rudimentary versions of Chinese characters. There are five thousand different kinds of characters on the bones, and so far they have deciphered about one thousand five hundred. From these they have been able to work out that the bones were used for getting advice from the gods. Each bone – typically shoulder blades of deer and oxen, or tortoise carapaces – had a question, about the prospects of everything from harvests to battles, and an answer, found by interpretation of the cracks that appeared when the bone was heated. Since they also mention the need for the Shang to worship their Xia ancestors, it is hard to believe the Xia didn't exist.

Zhou dynasty
1045–221 BCE

After five centuries of Shang rule, in the eleventh century BCE, a warlike people called the Zhou swept into the Yellow River valley from the Wei valley in the west, led by King Wen, King Wu and Wu's brother the duke of Zhou. So effective was their attack that they drove the Shang from power and took control of much of northern China. Interestingly, there was a fair amount of angst about whether it was morally right for the Zhou to take over like this. So the Zhou came up with the idea of the Mandate of Heaven, which has influenced the Chinese view of their rulers ever since. The basic idea is that rulers receive their mandate to rule from heaven – but if they misbehave, they lose the mandate and can therefore be deposed. Naturally, the Zhou emphasised the goodness, unselfishness and restraint of Kings Wen and Wu and the Duke of Zhou.

The Zhou dynasty is by far the longest in Chinese history, surviving for over eight hundred years, but it is divided into several periods. The first, lasting three centuries and called the Western Zhou, showed the Zhou at their strongest, ruling from Xi'an and Luoyang over Shaanxi, Shanxi and Hebei. But in 771 BCE, a tribe of horse nomads drove in from the West, maybe helped by disaffected subjects, took Xi'an and killed the Zhou King You. Feudal lords then set up one of his sons as King Ping in the eastern capital Luoyang.

The collapse of the Western Zhou led to a long period in which China was split between countless small states. The Zhou dynasty continued to exist, so the period is called

Eastern Zhou, but their power was sapped. Warfare was constant, and there was none of the stability of either earlier or later periods. And yet it was a time of intellectual ferment and technical innovation. Indeed, many of the central ideas of Chinese culture and many of its early inventions arose in this time. In some ways, it was the very instability that spurred people to think and invent and trade, as they sought to come to terms with the shifting sands around them. Interestingly, most of the great technological breakthroughs of the early Chinese, such as the invention of steel, came not from the 'refined' central states such as Zhou, Song and Lu, but from the more 'barbarous' peripheral states such as Qi in the east, Chu in the south and Qin in the west. But it is not the inventions that the period is really celebrated for but the great philosophical ideas that emerged out of the turmoil, as thinkers tried to work out just why times were so troubled.

Zhou thinking

There were four main strands of philosophy to emerge in the Easten Zhou period. The most famous was Confucianism, named after Confucius, the Roman name given by the Jesuits in the seventeenth century CE to the man his disciples knew as Kong Fuzi ('Master Kong'). Confucius's ideas have come down mainly in the form of sayings compiled by his followers in a tract called the Analects. His central belief was that we should seek to live in a good way, always behaving with humanity and courtesy, working diligently and honouring properly our family and our rulers. He thought of himself as a conservative in that he was always emphasising the 'Way of the Former Kings' in a previous Golden Age but in some ways, he was quite revolutionary in that he insisted status should be earned by moral behaviour and not by heredity. Politically, Confucianism championed a highly ordered society.

The second central philosopher of the age was Mo Zi. Mo Zi felt that Confucius's emphasis on the family could lead to nepotism and clan feuds. He argued in favour of 'universal love' – loving and honouring everyone, and looking after others as you would wish to be looked after yourself. This was not, he felt, an idealistic dream, but the only practical way for society to function without strife.

The third philosopy was Daoism (sometimes spelled as Taoism), with its central text, the *Dao De Jing* (The Book of the Way). Legend has it that it was written by someone called Lao Zi, but Lao Zi simply means 'Old Master' and it was probably written by several people. Lao Zi's solution to the troubles of the world is to do nothing. His belief is that strife arises because people are constantly striving, and so constantly coming up against opposition and obstacles. He didn't mean literally doing nothing, but going with the flow, like a stream running to the sea. 'The Way', the *Dao De Jing* says, 'never acts yet nothing is left undone'. Although nowadays people in the West associate the Way with a state of serenity that is totally apolitical, that is not how it was intended. The *Dao De Jing* says that rulers should get on with ruling with no regard to their people, leaving them ignorant and treating them 'like straw dogs' – which may be one reason why many rulers took up Daoism. It implied no responsibility of care for the populace.

The fourth Zhou period philosophy was in many ways the flipside to this political Daoism. This was the idea of Legalism. This advocated creating such a complete and rigid framework of law that there was no room for anyone to err. But for this to work, of course, those initiating the laws would have to take over all of China. If both Daoism and Legalism came to colour the thinking of Chinese emperors through the ages, maybe it influenced the attitude of the country's communist rulers, too.

Spring and Autumn

Just as the Zhou dynasty is divided into two periods, so the Eastern Zhou is divided into two periods, called the Spring and Autumn (770–464 BCE), and the Warring States (463–222 BCE), after the main historical accounts of the periods, known as the *Spring* and *Autumn Annals* and the *Strategies* of the *Warring States*.

Throughout both periods the myriad states that China had split into were constantly at war. At the beginning of the Eastern Zhou, there were 170 states, each vying at least for its own survival, if nothing more. No area was more fragmented into states than China's heartland. As the Zhou period went on, these small central states felt more and more threatened by the larger states on China's periphery, such as Chu, Wu and Qin. They felt they carried the flame of China's civilisation against these barbarians on the fringes, and called themselves *Zhongguo*, the Central Kingdoms, which is what Chinese people call their country today. Yet these Central Kingdoms became so absorbed in squabbling with each other that they barely noticed these rough outsiders gaining ground.

Wars were an almost constant feature of the period, especially among the Central Kingdoms, and as the states vied for control gradually numbers were whittled down to just a handful. Meanwhile one renegade from the state of Wei, a high-ranking official called Shang Yang – presumably finding his ideas falling on deaf ears at home – decided to take Legalism to Qin. He quickly found favour with the ruler of Qin and began to establish there a rigid hierarchy of status, and a tight legal framework for ownership and duties. Shang Yang's reforms turned Qin into an incredibly well-organised, centralised state, with an army to match. Gradually, in the century after 318 BCE, Qin became so powerful that it was strong enough to engulf more and more states. By 221 BCE, their conquest of all the northern states was complete and the Qin king Zheng changed his name to Shi Huangdi, the First Emperor, and China was united for the first time under a single ruler.

Shi Huangdi and Qin
221–206 BCE

Shi Huangdi was clearly a powerful and charismatic man, and he threw himself into ruling his new empire with a vengeance. Welding the patchwork of states and cultures into a whole demanded a certain ruthlessness, and Shi Huangdi was equal to it. Within a few years, Shi Huangdi had imposed a uniform Legalistic framework right across the empire, and divided it into 36 (later 48) military districts with a rigid hierarchy of officials governing each. Weights and measures and, most significantly, writing, were updated and standardised, establishing the characters still used today.

At the same time, Shi Huangdi became determined to guard his empire against threats from without as well as chaos from within. The main outside threat came from the steppe peoples to the north. Short earth ramparts already provided some protection, but Shi Huangdi decided to unify them all in one Great Wall stretching right across the north of the empire. With the forced labour of tens of thousands of peasants, this first Great Wall, built of rammed earth, was erected in barely five years.

But despite all Shi Huangdi's efforts, dissent persisted, and scholars began to protest against the harsh yoke of Legalism. The scholarly arguments became so vociferous that the emperor decided to burn all books outside his own library, except books on entirely practical matters such as medicine and agriculture. This measure earned Shi Huangdi the lasting hatred of Confucian scholars, but it failed to quell the resistance to Legalistic ideas.

In 210 BCE, Shi Huangdi died and was given a burial suited to his immense power. In 1974, workmen digging a well in Lintong outside Xian discovered some life-sized models of ancient warriors made of terracotta. When archaeologists began to explore the site, they discovered a vast necropolis under an artificial hill. Since then a staggering army of seven thousand of these terracotta warriors has been found, each one with its own unique face, along with bronze horses and chariots and much more. Amazingly, the best is yet to come, for archaeologists have yet to unearth Shi Huangdi's burial chamber, thought to be full of awesome riches.

With Shi Huangdi gone, though, the Qin empire quickly descended into chaos, as various Qin lords vied to be emperor. Popular revolts against Qin rule began to break out after a peasant named Chen She refused to be conscripted to the Qin army, and aristocratic opposition began to revive in the Chu state, always the main rival to Qin. In 206 BCE, a Chu lieutenant named Liu Bang, who had once been a bandit chief, led an army to defeat the third (and last) Qin emperor, and then, like a Chinese Oliver Cromwell, turned on his own lord and declared himself emperor Gao Zu, the first emperor of a new dynasty, the Han, which was to rule China for four centuries.

The Han
206 BCE–220 CE

Gao Zu was very much a man of the people and kept his bluff country ways even in the midst of court life. Indeed, he prided himself on his plain, no-nonsense approach. The power of the old aristocracy, which had prevailed under the Zhou, was banished for ever and the harsh totalitarianism of the Qin was abandoned in favour a gentler Confucianism as the empire's guiding philosophy. The tax burden on all but merchants was reduced, and state interference in trade was lessened in keeping with Confucianist ideals.

Gradually, too, the old feudal gentry were removed from the centres of power, as they were replaced by a class of officials who earned their place entirely on merit.

But Gao Zu was a pragmatist, not an idealist, and he was happy to maintain much of the Qin's standardisation and centralised grip on power. To prevent another military takeover like his own, he handed out large tracts of the country to his relatives.

The mixture seemed to work well, and the Han dynasty presided over the first great Chinese cultural flowering, when Chinese art and ideas began to bloom to an unprecedented extent. With a new-found confidence, the Chinese began to swell their frontiers and trade across the world in both ideas and goods. Indeed, this period so defined the core of Chinese culture that even today the name for the ethnic and cultural group that makes up the vast majority of Chinese people is called Han Chinese.

Liu Bang lived barely a decade after making himself emperor, but the rule he established proved so durable that it survived a number of challenges, and a number of short-lived emperors until the sixth Han emperor, Wu Di came to power in 141 BCE. Wu Di was known as the Martial Emperor, and he lived up to his name. He was dynamic and fiercely ambitious. One of his first acts was to shake up and streamline government. Instead of numerous officials, he set up an office of 'palace writers' or clerks to issue a stream of edicts to all the arms of the government and to control which of the multitude of documents the government received actually reached the emperor. He also took the idea of appointing officials on merit to its logical Confucian conclusion by establishing a national university to train officials, with entry by competitive examination. He issued this famous announcement:

'Heroes wanted! A proclamation!

Exceptional work demands exceptional men. A bolting or kicking horse may eventually become a most valuable animal. A man who is the object of the world's detestation may live to accomplish great things. As with the intractable horse, so with the detested man – it is simply a matter of training.

We therefore command the various district officials to search for men of brilliance and exceptional talent, to be OUR generals, OUR ministers, and OUR envoys to distant states.'

(From Giles, Gems of Chinese Literature*)*

Not content with setting up a civil service, which even today is a model for civil services around the world, Wu Di was determined to expand the empire's borders. By the time he died in 87 BCE, after 54 years in power, Wu Di had not only swelled the empire to include many of the western and south-western states, but had also sent a famous military expedition under General Li Guangli as far as modern Kazakhstan. Under the watchful eye of the Han armies, the legendary Silk Road trade route was established to allow merchants to carry Chinese silk, spices and tea right across Central Asia and all the way to Rome.

Over the century after Wu Di's death, though, the Han empire's resources were becoming stretched, and the court was being undermined by political intrigue. In 9 CE, Wang Mang seized the throne from the Hans. Wang Mang was an ardent Confucianist and reinstituted what he saw as the titles and institutions of the Zhou 'Golden Age'. Astonishingly, in a move that anticipated Mao by almost two millennia, he decided to nationalise all land and redistribute it to the peasants. Unfortunately, the move ran into powerful opposition from landowners. When disastrous floods also wrecked the harvest before Wang Mang could find a way to redistribute the land, a band of peasants known as the Red Eyebrows (because they painted their faces red like demons) revolted, too. Opposition from both the aristocracy and the peasantry proved too much for Wang Mang and he was driven from power by another strong Han leader, Guang Wu Di (Shining Martial Emperor).

Han rule was restored, but the empire's best days were past. Gradually, the empire began to crumble, as generals and regional leaders began to carve out their own territories. China was continually wracked by civil wars, and peasant uprisings, such as the Yellow Turbans and the Five Pecks of Rice Band of Sichuan and Shaanxi, who tried to abolish private property. Despite this turmoil, though, Chinese culture still flourished. Both Confucianism and Daoism developed strongly, and were joined by Buddhism, which began to enrich Chinese life and arts with a new way of thinking. Technology advanced, too, with things such as the watermill, the wheelbarrow, water clocks, seismographs to monitor earthquakes, and armillary spheres to plot the movements of the stars and planets all making their appearance.

Three Kingdoms and Sui
220–618 CE

In 220 CE, the Han empire finally collapsed, and for the next four centuries, China was split by a seemingly endless war between three rival states, Wei, Wu and Shu, earning this period the name of Three Kingdoms. Yet, despite the strife, Chinese culture continued to flourish, as it had under the later Hans, and when general Yang Jian finally unified China to found the Sui dynasty as Emperor Wen in 581 CE, the country was prosperous and richly cultured.

Wen established his capital at Chang'an in the north of China, but China's grain basket was now along the Yangtze River, over 2,000 kilometres (1,200 miles) away. Moving huge quantities of grain in carts over rutted roads was proving impractical, so Wen's Sui successor Yang Di began a building project to beat even the Great Wall in magnitude – the Grand Canal to link the Yangtze and the Yellow River. This extraordinary project was completed in just a year, thanks to the forced labour of five-and-a-half million people. But in the course of the work well over two million people died and, to add insult to slaughter, Yang Di swanned up and down the canal in his 100-kilometre-long (60 miles) 'dragon fleet' with its giant four-deck floating palace for him and his concubines, hauled by eighty thousand peasants. Not surprisingly, Yang Di was not much liked, and in 618 he was assassinated in a revolt led by General Li Yuan who became the first Tang emperor Gao Zu, the same name that Liu Bang had chosen when he became the first Han emperor.

Medieval China: Tang and Song
618–1278

The Tang dynasty was perhaps the high point of ancient Chinese culture. While Europe was plunged into the Dark Ages, China flourished as never before. At a time when few cities in Europe had populations numbering more than tens of thousands, and most buildings were little more than shabby huts, China boasted more than two dozen cities with populations of more than half a million – many of them sophisticated, cosmopolitan places with gardens, tea houses, taverns and restaurants, and comfortable, gracious houses for the middle class. With agricultural yields high, hunger was rare, and the wealthy had a life of rich leisure, replete with pedigree horses, trained hawks, polo, chess, silks, spices, perfumes and beautiful porcelain.

It was a cosmopolitan society, too, and some twenty-five thousand foreigners lived in the capital Xi'an, which is estimated to have had a population of two million – something not matched in Europe until London in the nineteenth century. Chinese confidence was at a high point, and they sent traders and travellers out all over the world to gather new ideas to add to the wealth of their society. The Silk Road was at its busiest, but the sea route to the west thrived, too, and Arab and Persian trading ships frequently docked in Guangzhou, while Chinese ships sailed to the Persian Gulf. The traveller Xuan Zang spent sixteen years travelling round India and brought back a wealth of knowledge about Buddhism, which by this time was a powerful force in Chinese society.

China's lead in technology, too, was at its most marked in the time of the Tangs and the Songs. During this medieval period, books began to be printed with movable type. Gunpowder was used to create devastating weapons of war. Oil was drilled from wells deep underground and piped through bamboo pipes. Magnets were used for compasses as well as astrological divination. And while Europeans were still sailing in small boats with a single mast and single sail, the Chinese were building huge, multi-masted, multi-sailed junks bigger than anything to be built in Europe for another five hundred years.

Interestingly, the Tangs had China's only empress, Wu Zetian, who ruled China with an iron hand for fifty years, from 655 to 705. Wu introduced a number of key reforms, including opening up the civil service to poor scholars, and insisting women take part in rites previously reserved for men, and oversaw the building of many Buddhist monuments including the famous Longmen carvings near Luoyang. But she had a reputation for ruthlessness, and by 705, she faced so much opposition that she was forced to abdicate.

When Wu went, the confidence of the Tang dynasty seemed to go, too. The following two centuries saw the country begin to fragment into various regional and political alliances, and the country became more and more vulnerable to attacks from the north. By 907, the Tang had gone. Over the next half century, power see-sawed between Five Dynasties in the north and Ten Kingdoms in the south, until in 960, the army finally put a general, Song Tai Zu, on the imperial throne to found the Song dynasty, which lasted until 1278.

The first half of the Song dynasty is known as the Northern Song, because the emperors ruled from Kaifeng on the Yellow River in the north. But in 1115, the Jurched people of Manchuria drove the Song emperors out of the north to re-establish one of the Five Dynasties, the Jin. The Song moved south and ruled from Huangzhou.

The loss of the north was a considerable blow to the Song, but it was not an absolute disaster, for by this time, the south was as developed as the north and the farming land of Yangtze valley and the Pearl River delta was the richest in China. Hangzhou grew to become as great a city as Xi'an had been under the Tangs, as Marco Polo testified when he visited in the thirteenth century after the Song had gone.

The time of the Khans
1278–1368

With the Jin and the Song occupied with each other, they perhaps failed to appreciate what was going on to the north amongst the Mongol peoples. After long being divided amongst various fiefdoms, the Mongols were united in 1206 under Temujin, who became Genghis Khan, which meant 'Universal Ruler'. Genghis Khan proved to be a hugely effective military leader and with his skilled horsemen to help him he embarked on a series of conquests that outshone even Alexander the Great, one of the most successful military commanders in history. Tibet and the Tarim Basin fell swiftly to the Mongol marauders. In 1209, they overran the Uighur region. Then, in 1210, they stormed into Jin China in the north and were soon ravaging it with their trademark wanton carnage. The Song in the south delighted in their rivals' plight, perhaps little thinking what it could mean in the long term. By 1234, the Mongols under Genghis Khan's son Ogedai Khan took the city of Kaifeng to deliver all Jin China in their hands, and the last Jin emperor committed suicide.

For a while, the Mongol aggression in China died down as Ogedai concentrated his efforts on Vietnam and Europe where the Mongols had reached Poland and Hungary. But the respite was brief. When Genghis Khan's grandson Kublai became Khan in the 1250s, the Mongol assault in China resumed. In 1260, Kublai became the great Khan, built a new city, the 'Tartar City' of Beijing, and declared himself Emperor of China, founding the Yuan dynasty. Within a few years, the Song had crumbled and Kublai Khan was ruler of a vast empire stretching right across Asia, from Moscow to the Indus and from the Mediterranean to the Pacific.

Under Kublai Khan and his Yuan successors, China once again experienced peace. Surprisingly, the Mongols quickly lost their wild ways in China, and took on Chinese habits, and the Yuan proved as effective rulers as China had had for centuries. The vast extent of the empire also made it much easier for a host of foreign travellers, including Marco Polo, to visit and see the magnificence of the new city of Beijing. Interestingly, a Russian came top of the Civil Service exams in 1341. But there was always simmering resentment, not just from the Chinese officials who retired to their country homes to paint and read, but also ordinary Chinese people, too, who found the power of the foreign Mongols more oppressive than that of their own native emperors. Throughout the fourteenth century, rebellions became more and more frequent, and in 1368, after a revolt in the Yangtze, monk-turned-bandit-leader Zhu Yuanzhang, calling himself Prince of Wu, seized the throne from the last Yuan boy emperor.

Ming and Qing
1368–1840

Wu became the first emperor of the Ming dynasty, ruling from Nanjing (the modern-day capital of Jiangsu province). The Ming united China under Chinese rule again for the first time since the Tang, but Wu proved far more ruthless than any of the Yuan, killing thousands of civil servants and academics in a series of purges. The impact of this, following a century of foreign rule, robbed the Chinese of their confidence, and Chinese culture began to become increasingly inward-looking and conservative, a tendency that became even more pronounced under the Qing dynasty that followed in 1644.

Indeed China became so introverted that it hardly noticed as European explorers sailed round the world; and as European science and technology not only caught up with but far outstripped anything that China could offer. Thus when the British Lord MacCartney led a huge delegation to China in 1793 to negotiate a trading partnership, he was rejected out of hand by the Qing emperor who felt the rest of the world had nothing to offer, and he would not make an alliance with what he viewed as a minor nation.

Unfortunately for the Qing, the Europeans were not

prepared to take no for an answer, perceiving that a nation as populous and as fabulously endowed as China was said to be must offer rich trading possibilities. Since the seventeenth century, demand had been growing in China for opium. Most of it had been home grown, but British traders had a ready source of opium in British India and were soon shipping in boatloads of Indian opium to China to satisfy Chinese demand. The trade was illegal, of course – not because of any moral disapproval of drugs, but because of trade restrictions on foreign goods. That didn't stop the British traders, however, who simply weighed anchor off Guangzhou and sold their cargo to local Chinese dealers who ran the opium ashore in fast boats to evade the authorities, who turned something of a blind eye. Meanwhile, British ships sped tea, silk and porcelain back to England to satisfy a growing taste for tea and chinoiserie.

Some high-ranking Qing officials, many of whom were opium smokers, pushed to legalise the opium trade. But the Qing emperor felt that opium was robbing the country of the silver that tea and other exports brought in, and from 1837 ordered officials to stamp out the trade. In 1839, Lin Zexu, governor of Guangzhou, seized all the opium held by European merchants in warehouse vessels offshore – out of Chinese jurisdiction. The British foreign secretary Lord Palmerston immediately ordered a British fleet and four thousand troops to China, beginning the first Opium War. After two years of shelling from British gunboats, the Chinese were forced to accept the opening of Chinese ports to trade, and the ceding of Hong Kong to the British to act as a trading base.

The end of the empire
1840–1911

The humiliation of foreign defeat and growing economic hardship in the country sapped the Qings of their authority. On the outside, China yielded ever more territory and influence to the European powers. On the inside, the Chinese people, facing a breakdown of traditional hierarchies and increasing poverty, began to challenge the Qing. The final straw was the country's defeat in 1895 in a war with Japan. In response, young radicals started 'Revive China' and 'Self-strengthening' campaigns, and in October that year the China Revival Society, a republican society set up in 1894 by Guangdong doctor Sun Yat-sen, organised a plot to install a republican government in Guangzhou. The plot failed and many of the China Revival Society were killed or imprisoned. Sun Yat-sen escaped to London, where he was kidnapped by Qing officials before being released after pressure from the British.

Meanwhile in China, in 1899, a highly xenophobic martial arts sect called the Boxers decided the ills of the country were all down to foreigners. They began attacking and tearing down everything that could be remotely construed as foreign, from Christian missions to railway lines laid by European companies. The Qing empress Cixi wavered then decided to support the Boxers. As foreigners were besieged in Beijing, a multinational force arrived to protect them. Cixi fled Beijing in a cart, disguised as a peasant.

By now the Qing's authority was gone, and though Empress Cixi returned to Beijing in 1902, it was only a matter of time before the end came. In 1908, Cixi died, leaving her two-year-old nephew Pu Yi as the last emperor. In 1911, opposition to foreign-owned railways came to a head, and an uprising in Wuchang in Hubei ignited a popular rebellion, which finally pulled down the dying empire. On 29 December that year, republican revolutionary Sun Yat-sen was elected provisional president of the new republic of China by a congress of delegates from sixteen regional assemblies.

The Chinese Republic
1911–1921

It was not Sun Yat-sen, though, who held the real power in China. The man who was really master of China at that time was General Yuan Shikai. Yuan had all the military behind him, and in October 1911, the Qing courtiers had appointed him premier. The scene was now set for a civil war between Yuan and the Qing on one hand and the republican revolutionaries on the other. To avoid strife both sides entered negotiations and it was proposed that if Yuan would agree to be president of the new republic of China, he would support the republic and force the boy Qing emperor to abdicate. When Sun Yat-sen was elected president, Yuan at once withdrew from negotiations. Faced with an agonising choice, Sun Yat-sen stepped down and a new republican government was set up in Beijing with Yuan as president.

Although the government adopted a constitution, in reality, Yuan pulled all the strings, and he did not hesitate to use them. To try and curb his power, the revolutionaries formed a political party, the Guomindang (the GMD or Nationalist Party). But when the GMD won a landslide victory in the 1912 elections, Yuan dismissed the parliament, outlawed the GMD and began to rule through the military. In the summer of 1913, seven southern provinces declared independence, and Yuan sent in his armies to swiftly crush this 'Second Revolution', forcing Sun Yat-sen into exile.

Yuan clearly had higher ambitions than merely being president. Just as so many military leaders had done before in Chinese history, Yuan planned to set himself up as the first emperor of a new dynasty. But before he could be inaugurated, he died. Sun Yat-sen returned again to establish a Nationalist government in the south in Guanghzhou, while the warlords and generals ruled the roost in the north and various provinces.

But during the time China had been divided and the western powers had been preoccupied with the First World War, Japan had taken advantage of the situation to issue 'Twenty-One Demands' to China, which would give Shandong to Japan and make China virtually a Japanese protectorate. In a weak position, Yuan had been forced to accept a modified version of these demands in 1915, but with the First World War over, the Chinese hoped the West would put pressure on Japan to back down. Instead, at the Treaty of Versailles in 1919, France and the USA, who had already signed secret pacts with Japan, withdrew their support for China. The previous decade had seen a tremendous ferment of ideas among the young, and a real excitement about the political ideals of the West. For them, the Versailles decision was a crushing blow. When news came through on 4 May 1919, three thousand students from Beijing University took to the streets in protest. The Beijing authorities suppressed the demonstrators and jailed the leaders, but this only served to spark off a wave of protests around the country.

The Red rebellion
1921–1949

Inspired by events in Russia, some of the protestors joined together to form the Chinese Communist Party (CCP) in 1921, with leaders such as Mao Zedong and Zhou Enlai. Encouraged by their Russian backers, who had argued with Marx that before a revolution of the masses China needed to have a bourgeois revolution, the CCP joined forces with the GMD in its fights against the northern warlords. But when Sun Yat-sen died in 1925, he was succeeded by his brother-in-law and young military chief Chiang Kaishek. Unlike the socialist Sun Yat-sen, Chiang Kaishek had little time for the Communists and was suspicious of their Russian support. Expelled from the GMD, the CCP was forced underground. In 1928, they organised a strike in Shanghai, which was crushed so violently by Chiang Kaishek's troops that five thousand workers and communists were killed. The GMD came increasingly to be seen as on the side of China's elite.

While most Communists worked in the cities to organise opposition, Mao went to the country to mobilise the peasants, who he felt were the key to the revolution. He organised the first peasant army, called the Red Army, in Jiangxi province.

At first, the Red Army had some success, using guerilla strikes out of the mountains. Then Chiang Kaishek encircled them in the Jinggang Shan with an army half-a-million strong. The Red Army, with just eighty thousand men and little equipment would have no chance in a battle, so in October 1934, Mao organised an epic retreat over 9,500 kilometres (6,000 miles) through the mountains, which came to be known as the Long March. By the time the Red Army reached their northern base at Yan'an in Shaanxi a year later, they had lost three-quarters of their strength through cold, starvation and desertion. But this epic feat earned the CCP the respect of many Chinese people and made Mao undisputed Communist leader.

Meanwhile the Japanese were becoming more and more aggressive and, in July 1937, they launched an attack on Beijing. Chiang Kaishek insisted that his first priority was to defeat the Communists, but his subordinates disagreed and forced him to join with the CCP in a United Front against the Japanese. Even together, though, the GMD and the CCP were no match for the Japanese, who swiftly occupied all of eastern China from Beijing to Guanzhou. The United Front withdrew to Chongqing in Sichuan, where their unity swiftly evaporated.

With the attack on Pearl Harbor, Japan made an enemy of the USA, and put America on the side of the Chinese. When Japan was finally defeated in 1945, the Japanese were forced to withdraw from China. The situation they left behind them, though, was chaotic. During the war, countless people had joined the Red Army to drive out the Japanese, so when the Japanese left, most of the territories they had occupied were

'Liberated Areas' under Communist control, and the Red Army was almost a million strong. The scene was set for a massive showdown between the GMD and the CCP.

Civil war broke out in Manchuria, and although a temporary peace was brokered by the US general George Marshall, it was short-lived. The tide began to turn in the Communists' favour. In 1948, the Communist army, now renamed the People's Liberation Army (PLA) defeated the GMD in a huge battle at Hua Huai. As the PLA advanced towards Shanghai, Chang Kaishek realised the cause was lost and fled to Taiwan to form the Republic of China, waiting there with the two million troops and refugees who later joined him with the forlorn hope of one day liberating the mainland. In October 1949, Mao proclaimed the founding of the People's Republic of China to make China the most populous Communist country by far.

Mao's China
1949-1976

Most Chinese welcomed the People's Republic warmly, not necessarily because they were Communists but because the country was finally united under one rule, and because the civil wars were at an end. But in line with the approach of the Stalinists in Russia, the CCP moved swiftly to neutralise opposition. Tens of thousands of supporters of the GMD were executed or sent to labour camps, intellectuals were forcibly enrolled in 'criticism and self-criticism' classes, the press and the expression of opinion in public were curtailed, foreign missionaries were forced to leave the country, and a million or some say even two million landlords were put to death so that the land would be free for redistribution. Significantly, the elimination of the landlords destroyed the gentry, the class that had always dominated Chinese government. It was clear who was in charge now.

At first, the redistributed land was not taken out of private ownership but simply spread among the peasants who were each given a plot of land as their own. The peasants went to work on their own land with extraordinary enthusiasm and within a few years agricultural output was higher than it had ever been. At the same time, the CCP nationalised industry and enlisted former business owners to manage state-owned companies. The first of a series of Five-Year Plans (1953–58) emphasised heavy industry, and the country's industrial output rose steadily.

By the mid-1950s, however, some of the initial euphoria was lost. There was considerable debate on how the country should move forward. They agreed the ultimate aim was a Communist country, but what they couldn't agree on was how to get there. The first Five-Year Plan accepted a gradual approach, and was called afterwards the Little Leap Forward. Rural households were urged to band together into ever larger co-operative units providing 'mutual aid' – first twenty to forty household units, then one to three hundred households.

Mao, though, was impatient and was determined to drive things on. In 1957, he loosened the restrictions on the expression of opinions and actually encouraged the voicing of complaints with the slogan, 'Let a hundred flowers bloom, and a hundred schools of thought contend.' Mao said afterwards that he had expected people to point the finger at inefficient officials to get things moving. Instead, the Hundred Flowers campaign opened the way for intellectuals to criticise the CCP. Apparently incensed, Mao launched an anti-rightist campaign under Deng Xiaoping to silence the 'critics'. Half a million or more were purged by execution, exile to labour camps or a long dose of self-criticism. Some commentators now think Mao's Hundred Flowers campaign was just a ploy to flush out any critics of his next plan.

The Great Leap Forward
1958–1961

Mao's big idea was the Great Leap Forward. This was the name given to the second Five-Year Plan, from 1958–63, though now it has come to refer to just the first three years, from 1958 to 1961. Mao believed that with a massive concerted effort in both agriculture and industry, China could take a Great Leap Forward to economic prosperity and Communism. The two pillars of economic development, Mao was convinced, were steel and grain, and so the plan focused on a huge surge in steel and grain production to be achieved by everybody pulling together in a process of mass collectivisation.

In August 1958, the CCP's Politburo decided that there was to be no more private ownership of land. Instead, it was to be pooled into People's Communes run by party members, each based on an average of five thousand households. The idea was to turn small-scale peasant farms into efficient agricultural units in one fell swoop. Peasants were moved away from their homes and dragooned into production brigades and production teams where they would work not for money but work units. Children were to be looked after separately while their parents lived and worked on the commune. There was even a plan to put everyone in large communal eating halls and dormitories, but this idea was quickly dropped in the face of widespread opposition. Astonishingly, within a few months, twenty-five thousand communes had been set up, covering most of the country.

At the same time, Mao drove forward a plan to boost industrial production massively by a collective effort. Steel, coal and electricity output were to swell by more than a third each year so that, Mao argued, within ten years, China's industrial output would match Britain's and within fifteen years it would overtake that of the USA. Seasonally employed workers were, for instance, to be co-opted by the million to build heavy industrial plants, dig canals and drain marshes. The centrepiece of Mao's plan, however, was that every commune should have its own backyard steel furnace to make steel from scrap iron.

The Great Leap Forward turned out to be a catastrophe. Agricultural yields slumped terribly on all the communal farms. One of the problems was that communes had been directed to plant grains in places better suited to other crops. Another was the directives, deriving from the Soviet pseudo-scientist Trofim Lysenko, to plant grains close together with the result that they became choked, and to plough deep, which buried the fertile topsoil. On nearly every commune, party members with no experience of farming tried to organise workers with no enthusiasm for the task. To make matters worse, farm workers were dragged into working the backyard blast furnaces at harvest time, leaving crops rotting in the ground. To cap it all, most of the grain harvest was shipped off to the cities to meet production quotas, regardless of whether rural workers had enough to eat. All this coincided with a combination of floods and droughts. The result was that China's rural population suffered its worst famine ever. Although estimates vary, it is thought that thirty million or more people died during the Great Leap Forward. Afterwards, the CCP decided that the famine had been 70 per cent policy failure and 30 per cent natural disaster.

The industrial drive proved equally disastrous economically, though not in human terms. The concentration on steel production meant that every other industry suffered, and China's industrial output dropped by a half between 1958 and 1959. To make matters worse, the steel from the backward furnaces was so impure as to be virtually useless.

Mao accepted he was to blame for the disaster of the Great Leap Forward and resigned as chairman of the Republic, making way for Liu Shaoqi to become chairman, Zhou Enlai to become premier and Deng Xiaoping secretary. Mao remained chairman of the Chinese Communist Party, however, and it was only a matter of time before he made his comeback.

The Cultural Revolution
1966–1971

If Mao had given China a shock with the Great Leap Forward, the Great Proletarian Cultural Revolution was, if anything, an even bigger shock. Mao's avowed aim was to rid the country of bourgeois ideas and recapture the early zeal of Communism by mobilising the country's youth, but it was clear he also wanted to get rid of his opponents in the party. Urged on by Mao, students at Beijing University began to agitate against university and government officials who they claimed were too bourgeois. When Liu Shaoqi tried to damp down the agitation, Mao immediately launched a stinging public attack on him, and guided the students to form their own political militia, the Red Guard. At the same time, Mao's supporters encouraged the growth of a personality cult around Mao by distributing copies of his sayings in his *Little Red Book*.

The Red Guard swelled dramatically and schools and universities across China closed down as young Red Guards took to the streets to target the Four Olds – old ideas, old culture, old customs and old habits. Academics were assaulted, books were burned, temples and monuments were attacked, shops selling anything remotely western were burned to the ground, and the gardens of the bourgeoisie were ripped to shreds. Government officials right up to the top, including Liu Shaoqi and Deng Xiaoping, were driven from office. Tens of thousands of people were beaten up, abused, killed or driven to suicide as the campaign rolled on. As fighting broke out among Red Guard factions and the country was beginning to descend into lawlessness, Mao finally yielded to pressure. He sent in the military, which took control and rounded up millions of young Red Guards and sent them off to the country, reportedly to preach the Communist message to the rural community.

In 1969, Mao was re-elected as chairman of the Republic amid great fanfare, and Lin Biao was named as his successor. Lin was Mao's personal choice and best student, and yet, according to the CCP, he at once turned against Mao, plotted unsuccessfully to assassinate him and was then killed in an air crash over Mongolia while trying to flee to Russia.

The deaths of Zhou and Mao and the rise of Deng 1971–1978

Throughout the Cultural Revolution, though, one figure had seemed to remain above it – the much-loved Zhou Enlai. Zhou Enlai is believed to have used his influence to moderate the worst effects of the Cultural Revolution and heal some of the wounds afterwards. He is also believed to have been behind the new move towards friendship with the USA, which culminated in the famous visit of President Richard Nixon to China in 1971 and 1972 – helping to gain the People's Republic recognition as the state of China, replacing Taiwan at the United Nations. Zhou Enlai believed it was essential for China to take her place as a major world state and to achieve equal status by genuine internal development, involving 'four modernisations' – agriculture, industry, science and technology, and defence.

Mao attacked Zhou as being 'rightist' but Zhou survived, only to become gravely ill with cancer in 1973. With Mao's approval, Deng Xiaoping took over from Zhou and carried on with his four modernisations. But when Zhou died amidst general mourning in January 1976, Deng at once attracted vituperative attacks from four powerful figures within the party known as the Gang of Four – Mao's wife Jiang Qing, along with Wang Hongwen, Zhang Chunqiao and Yao Wenyuan. Deng was stripped of all his official positions and Mao selected the relatively unknown Hua Guofeng to become premier. For a month or so it seemed as if the Gang of Four would reverse all Zhou's reforms. On 5 April 1976, two million people gathered in Tiananmen Square in Beijing to mourn the passing of Zhou Enlai, and the assembly turned into a protest against the Gang of Four.

On 9 September of that year, Mao also died and on his deathbed he had written to Hua, apparently, 'With you in charge, I'm at ease.' Hua became party chairman, and with Deng's and the army's support, he arrested the Gang of Four. Two years later, Deng returned to leadership yet again. Ostensibly he was deputy premier to his protégé Hu Yaobang, but it was eminently clear who was really in charge of China. Of the three original leaders of China's Communist Revolution – Mao, Zhou and Deng – it was Deng, the most unlikely of the three, who had survived and was to set China on the course it is taking now.

The landscape

China is a vast country, the third biggest in the world after Canada and Russia, and encompasses a vast array of different landscapes from the bleak deserts in the north to the lush tropical coast in the south. In simple terms, the country steps down from the gigantic mountains and high plateaux of the west, through the central hills and basins in the middle to the lowland plains and the coast to the east. The mountains provide the headwaters for three great rivers that flow east to the Pacific – the Huang He or Yellow River in the north, the Yangtze in the middle and the shorter Xi Jiang (Pearl River) in the south. Within that simple scheme, however, there is enormous variety.

China's north-east, once known as Manchuria, is made up of the three provinces of Heilongjiang, Jilin and Liaoning. Here, a great horseshoe of forested mountains encloses a fertile plain. To the west are the DA Xing'an Ling Mountains, arcing round into the Xiao Hing'an Ling and the Changbai Shan ranges in the east. Nearly all of the mountains are thickly wooded – one of the few areas of China to remain so – and they still provide the country's richest timber reserves. The black soils of the plains are rich agricultural land, farmed continuously for many thousands of years. Winters in Manchuria are bitter, with average temperatures plunging below –20°C (–4°F), yet the short hot summers, with their plentiful rainfall, allow crops of wheat, maize, millet, sunflowers and, especially, soya beans, to flourish.

The ancient heart of China is North China, bounded by the famous Great Wall in the north, and dominated by Beijing. In the west of the region, in the north of Shaanxi Province, is the Huangtu Gaoyuan, a vast plateau built up over millions of years by the wind whipping in fine dust from the deserts of Mongolia, and made famous in the film *Yellow Earth* (see page 276). Over time, the yellow earth or loess of the plateau has been sliced open with deep gulleys and sunken roads, but irrigation has allowed crops, cattle farms and forestry to thrive. To the south of the loess plateau lies the densely populated Weihe Plain where China's famous tea and sugar cane are grown in the south. To the east stretches the vast plains called the Huabei Pingyuan, traversed by the Yellow River. Humans have lived and worked here so long that much of the landscape is human-made, with almost every inch terraced or cultivated, except on the hills where deciduous forests still survive like islands in a dark sea. But lives here have often been marked with tragedy caused by the flooding of the Yellow River, sometimes called 'China's Sorrow' for the suffering it frequently brings.

To the north of the Great Wall lie the steppes of Inner Mongolia, stretching well over a thousand miles from the DA Xing'an Ling mountains in Heilonjiang to the Helan Shan range in the west. Some of this vast plateau is covered in grass. In other parts, there is so little rain that the land turns to *gobi* or stony desert. It is a harsh environment everywhere though; wind-blown and dry in summer, bitterly cold in winter. Crops such as cotton are grown in oases, where willow and poplar provide bursts of autumn colour. High on the northern steppes, traditional Mongol herders still rear sheep, cattle, camel and horses.

Beyond the Helan Shan, dry but fertile lands near the Yellow River merge imperceptibly into grasslands and then the arid wastes of Mongolia's Gobi desert, one of the harshest environments in the world, scorching hot in summer and icy cold in winter. Further still to the west lie the vast basins of Xinjiang so completely surrounded by high mountains that the region's few rivers can find no outlet to the sea but instead drain into lakes and swamps. There are three main basins or Pendi – the Junggar, the Tarim and the Turpan. Along the foothills of the mountains and by the rivers in the Junggar Pendi and the Turpan Pendi, the land is fertile enough to support agriculture, but water must be brought down from the mountains in underground channels to prevent evaporation in the hot sun. The Turpan, which at its lowest point is 160 metres (500 feet) below sea level, is famed for its melons and grapes. The Tarim Pendi, though, is so dry it is mostly filled by a vast sea of sand dunes, rearing up some 100 metres (330 feet), making up the Takla Makan desert – the driest region in all of Asia.

To the south of the Takla Makan ascend the lofty snow-capped peaks of the Kunlun Shan mountains. Climb over them and you reach what is sometimes called the 'Roof of the World', the Qinghai-Tibet Plateau. With an average elevation of over 4,000 metres (13,000 feet), it is the largest and highest mountain plateau in the world. It is surrounded on all sides by the world's highest peaks, with the crowning glories of the Himalayas in the south where Mount Everest or, as the

Chinese prefer Zhumulangma, soars to 8,850 metres (29,000 feet). Much of the landscape is bleak and barren, strewn with rocks and punctuated here and there with salt lakes and marshes. The weather here is cold and dry most of the year, with the biting winds and the rarefied air that only the hardy inhabitants feel comfortable breathing. Only in the southern valleys near the Yarlu Zangbu River is the climate milder and moister, and this is where most Tibetans live and farm.

The Qinghai-Tibet plateau is the source of many of Asia's greatest rivers including the Indus, the Ganga, the Brahmaputra, the Mekong, and China's Yellow River and Yangtze. From the Qinghai, the Yangtze flows down to the east for over six thousand kilometres (3,700 miles) to reach the sea near Shanghai, the longest river in Asia. The Yangtze and its tributaries drain over a fifth of all China's land area, and the Yangtze valley is in many ways the heartland of China. On its way to the sea, it flows through ruggedly beautiful mountains, gorges and broad basins, including the mountain-ringed Red Basin of Sichuan, named for its rich red soils. To the south, Yunnan and Guizhou form a vast plateau cut into island peaks by steep valleys. In Guizhou, the limestone has been dissolved by millennia of rain into a magical landscape of towering peaks, mist-shrouded spires and deep, quietly echoing gorges.

Further down the Yangtze to the east lies lowland China, intensively cultivated and densely populated. For thousands of years rice has been the main crop here, grown on low-terraced paddy fields. Tea is cultivated on the gentle hills that rise here and there above the plain. The plains are criss-crossed by countless waterways, including the ancient Grand

Canal, running from Hangzhou north to Beijing, and there are countless lakes, many topped up in the past each spring by snow meltwaters brought down by the Yangtze. What will happen when the gargantuan Three Gorges Dam closes in 2008 remains to be seen.

The south of China is subtropical and, on the island of Hainan, tropical. The climate is humid, with long, warm summers and mild winters. Summer monsoons bring plenty of rain and the temperatures are warm enough to grow two or even three crops during the year. But coastal regions are frequently lashed by summer typhoons that can wreak havoc with both high winds and flooding. Much of the coast is fringed by craggy mountains, which break at the sea into myriad natural harbours and offshore islands. Where rivers flow down, however, there are often broad, fertile floodplains – the biggest of which is the wide delta of the Xi Jiang (Pearl River) in Guangdong. In the past, the Pearl River delta was one of China's most productive agricultural regions, yielding huge quantities of rice, tubers and, especially, sugar cane – not to mention a cornucopia of fruit such as lychees, tangerines, pineapples and bananas. Now, however, it is better known as the focus of China's Industrial Revolution, and the site of the world's fastest growing megacity.

Wildlife

The sheer range of climates, soils and elevations in China, as well as its vast size, means China is home to a wider range of wild plants and animals than almost any other country in the world.

Plant life

There are an estimated 32,800 species of plants in China, a tenth of all the world's known plant species – half of them found in China and nowhere else on earth. In the north and west, there are grass and deserts, and countless flowers and herbs grow here as well as many kinds of grasses. In moister places, here and there, shrubs and even trees grow. But it is in the south and east that the real riches of China's flora lie.

About eight thousand years ago, trees would have cloaked most of the south and east in an almost unbroken forest stretching right from Hainan in the southwest to Heilongjiang in the north-east. Trees would have gradually changed in variety as you moved from the tropical south-west to the cool north-east and from the lowlands higher and higher up China's lofty mountains. In the tropical climes of the south-east would have been lush rainforests, full of a rich variety of tropical trees, including palms. But as you moved further north-east, or climbed higher up the mountain slopes, so the trees would have graded from rainforest to subtropical broad-leaf evergreen to broadleaf deciduous with oak, ash, elm and maple, not unlike New England in the US or southern England. Further up and further north-east, the deciduous trees would have given way to conifers such as larch.

No forested country has been cultivated for as long as China and the Chinese have had thousands of years to clear forest to make way for farms and provide fuel. Those vast ancient forests have now been stripped from nearly all lowland areas, and only survive in large forests on steep slopes and other less accessible spots.

The practice of herbal medicine testifies to the value Chinese people have always put on the prodigious diversity of natural plant species in these ancient woodlands, and about forty years ago – maybe earlier than most western countries – they began to realise what an effort they needed to make to preserve them. Over five thousand species are now in severe danger. In a scientific initiative remarkable for a Communist country, the Chinese government began to compile a complete province by province analysis of all the plants growing in China in the late 1960s. This resulted, thirty years later, in the gigantic 255-volume *Flora Sinica* (with a comparable series for animal life, the *Fauna Sinica*). Besides a systematic extension of nature reserves, China is in the process of setting up seed stores and botanical gardens, which are intended to preserve samples of eighteen thousand species of wild plants. In addition, they are beginning to breed hundreds of rare and endangered plant species such as *Cathaya argyronhylla* (a type of pine), *Metasequoia glyptostroboides* (the Dawn redwood) and *Davidia involucrate* (the handkerchief tree). In June 2007, the Chinese government announced a plan to let 15 million hectares of farmland to revert to forest by 2010 to protect biodiversity.

Plant-hunters, though, have long been aware just what a treasure trove China is. Over the last two hundred years, countless European and American botanists such as Reginald

Farrar and George Forest scoured the Chinese countryside – especially Gansu, Sichuan, Yunnan and Tibet – for plants to pot up and bring back home. So well did the specimens they collected thrive in their new homes, that many of the garden plants we now think of as familiar friends were actually transplants from China. Cherry trees, plum trees and gingkos all came from China, as did shrubs such as rhododendron, azalea and camellia, not to mention flowers such as deutzia, philadelphus, daphne, cotoneaster, forsythia, clematis and rose. Even delicate flowers such as gentian, primula, iris and saxifrage are Chinese immigrants. Go to the hills of Sichuan, and you will find most of these homely garden plants growing wild, often in great profusion.

Animal life

The diversity of China's fauna is even richer than its plant life. The great Domesday Book compilation of the nation's animal life, the *Fauna Sinica*, recorded 104,500 different species of animal life, more than any other single nation on earth. This is not just countless inconspicuous invertebrates, but the more spectacular vertebrates, too. China is home to at least 450 species of mammal – 13.5 per cent of the world total; 1,195 species of bird (11.2 per cent of the world total); 460 species of reptiles and amphibians; and about 2,000 species of fish.

All over the country, there are numerous small carnivores such as wolves, racoons, foxes and civets. In some areas, there are still small surviving clusters of larger carnivores – leopards and Amur tigers in the forests of the north-east, snow leopards in Tibet, and clouded leopards and Bengal tigers in the tropical south. The north-eastern forests, where winters are frequently bitter, are one of the few parts of China left untouched by man, and besides leopards and tigers, brown bear, sable, red deer and lynxes roam here beneath the trees. Perhaps the most stunning region for animal life, though, is Xishuangbanna, the southernmost part of Yunnan. Here in the tropical forests live 253 species of mammal – more than half of those in China. Besides clouded leopards and Bengal tigers, there are Indian elephants, gibbons, macaques and rare golden monkeys.

The symbol of China's wildlife, though, is the giant panda, now found only in Sichuan, Gansu and Shaanxi, where huge efforts are being made to help it survive in the world, with only moderate success. At every level of the Sichuan mountains a different range of animals find their home. Among the broadleaf evergreens and deciduous woods of the foothills live the rarest of all Chinese tigers, the South China tiger, as well as golden monkeys, and goatlike creatures such as serows and gorals. A little higher, among the mist-shrouded bamboo stands and the groves of pine and fir, dwell the giant pandas, along with the serows and gorals. Higher up still where the bamboos give way in the cooler air to thickets of rhododendron and azalea amid the pines, is home to Asiatic black bears, lynxes, tufted and muntjac deer, and oxlike takins. Above 3,000 metres (10,000 feet), where it is too cold even for pines to grow, the only large animals are lynx and tufted deer, but birds such as Reeves's pheasant make their home. Only the tufted deer makes it to the chilly, high alpine meadows above

4,000 metres (13,000 feet), where it is joined by birds such as the monal pheasant and the black-necked crane.

Endangered animals

A huge number of China's animal species are currently in danger. The biggest threat has been the loss of their habitats, but the Chinese taste for exotic animals both to eat and to use in traditional medicine has also taken its toll. The tiger has suffered particularly in this way, despite the trade in tiger parts being banned since 1993. There have been calls for China's five thousand captive tigers to be 'farmed' and their body parts sold for tiger-bone wine and other 'health-giving' concoctions. This, many Chinese argue, would save the wild tiger by reducing the need for poaching. Western conservationists, however, believe tiger farming would be a disaster, reviving demand for tiger parts that would encourage further poaching – especially since wild tigers are considered more 'potent'. With no more than five hundred adult tigers left in the wild in China, any increase in poaching would rapidly bring extinction. Indeed, the South China tiger may already be extinct in the wild, with no sightings since the late 1970s. The only remaining South China tigers are probably the 68 kept in Chinese zoos, all of which are the offspring of just 2 males and 4 females.

The giant panda does not suffer the same medicinal threats as the tiger, but its bamboo forest has been destroyed by farmers and loggers and its low reproduction rate has made it very vulnerable. There are fewer than one thousand pandas left in the wild, and desperate measures are afoot to save them. Even rarer, though less well loved, is the Chinese alligator, an ancient inhabitant of the Yangtze and a few other Chinese rivers. As development along the rivers accelerates, and the rivers become more and more polluted, so the alligator's survival is threatened. There are now fewer than five hundred Chinese alligator left in the wild.

Culture

Language

Over 90 per cent of Chinese people speak Chinese, the language of the I Ian people (the dominant ethnic group in China), which is the most widely spoken language on earth. That said, though, Han comes in various dialects, and those dialects are so different that in the past people speaking the Beijing dialect would find it as hard to understand someone from Guangzhou as a Portuguese would find it to understand someone from Romania – even though both Portuguese and Romanian are both Latin-based 'romance' languages. The words are often the same in the various Chinese dialects but both the tone with which they are spoken and the word order can be so different that they are mutually unintelligible. In the northern Chinese dialect (Mandarin), for instance, there are four different tones or pitches, which distinguish words that would otherwise sound the same. Southern Chinese has nine of these tones.

There are seven major dialects of Han Chinese. Six of them are spoken by fewer than 20 per cent of people in China including the Wu dialect of Shanghai and around (about 8 per cent), the Kejia (or Hakka Fujianese) dialect of Fujian (4 per cent), and the Yue (Cantonese) dialect of Hong Kong and Gunagzhou (5 per cent). Many of the vast diaspora of Chinese people around the world, especially in South-east Asia, also speak Cantonese or Fujianese. However, by far the most widely spoken dialect in mainland China now is Mandarin, spoken by some 70 per cent of Chinese people.

In the past, Mandarin was the language of officialdom and got its name from the Portuguese, who used the word to describe the dialect of the 'mandarins' (governors) of Beijing. Its use spread as government officials moved around the country and it paid people wherever they went to learn Mandarin in order to get on. In the 1950s, the government decided to promote its use as a common, national language and called it *putonghua* (which means 'common speech') rather than the foreign name 'mandarin'. *Putonghua* is the form of Chinese taught to foreigners and is the language Chinese children are taught in at school, the language of government and the language of the media such as the press and the Internet. In the major cities, almost every young person can read *putonghua* because they learned it at school. Not everyone who reads it, though, can necessarily speak it, and in rural areas knowledge of *putonghua* is much patchier.

Chinese characters

Interestingly, many of the vast differences between the different Chinese dialects vanish when they are written down.

The dialects may sound very, very different, but the words are written down with many of the same Chinese characters, so the sentence will mean the same whether the reader is from Beijing or Shenzhen. Because of the way Chinese characters work, they mean the same regardless of the way they are sounded – just as the written figure 4 means exactly the same whether you are French or German. All the same, most written Chinese is in the form of *putonghua* anyway. It is very rare to try and write any of the dialects down, except for Cantonese.

Chinese is the world's most complex written language. Whereas most of us in the West have just 26 letters to cope with, plus a few accent marks, Chinese has 50,000 or so characters. Highly educated Chinese people will probably be familiar with 10,000 of these, and anyone who is literate will know at least 2,500, which is what you need to know to read a newspaper.

The reason why there are so many characters written is because Chinese doesn't really work phonetically, so words cannot be built up from single sounds. Instead, there is a separate character for each word or syllable. Originally, written Chinese was based on simple graphic pictures (pictographs) of natural objects. There are pictographs like this dating back to the eleventh century BCE. Many written languages started like this and moved towards a phonetic alphabet, but Chinese characters only have a hint at pronunciation. Instead, as Chinese developed the language combined pictures to create new abstract meanings or ideographs. Thus a combination of the pictures for sun and moon meant 'bright' while a combination of the pictures for woman and child meant 'happiness'.

Tellingly, three pictures of women together meant 'treachery'. Chinese characters also developed as pictures came to be used for words that sounded the same when spoken. As an example, the picture character for an ear of corn developed into the character for the verb 'to come' because both words sound similar when spoken.

Several different writing styles developed as China split into different kingdoms between the seventh and third centuries BCE, but when the country was unified under the Qins in 221 BCE, the Qin style was imposed everywhere. The Qin style was substantially modified under the Han (206 BCE–220 CE), but modern Chinese characters are essentially no more than a development of the ancient Han characters.

Chinese characters look impossibly complex at first, but they are always made up from a particular number of strokes of the pen in a particular order. So the character for 'mouth', which is basically a square, is written with three strokes: first the left side, then the top and right together in a single stroke, and lastly the base. Typically, too, the character has two parts, with the right-hand side signifying the meaning in some way and the left, called the radical, signifying the sound. In the most common system, there are about 214 of these radicals, which are the closest thing Chinese has to western letters.

Written Chinese is hard even for Chinese children to learn and, in the 1950s, it was felt that this was holding back any improvements in literacy. So the government introduced two controversial measures. The first was to simplify the most commonly used few thousand characters, making them easier to learn and quicker to write. These simplified characters are now widely used in mainland China – although in places such as Hong Kong, the traditional characters are still used, and they are making something of a comeback among intellectuals on the mainland where they are seen as more sophisticated.

The second, even more drastic, measure was to try and dispense with Chinese characters altogether and instead write Chinese in the Roman alphabet. This 'romanised' Chinese was called *pinyin* and essentially involved using 25 letters of the western alphabet (excluding the letter 'v') to create the sounds of Mandarin Chinese along with accents above each syllable to create the four different tones. *Pinyin* never caught on in China, and the idea was quickly dropped, but *pinyin* is very useful for foreigners since it allowed any westerner, after a little basic instruction, to read and pronounce Chinese words without knowing any Chinese characters. It was the widespread adoption of *pinyin* that led to the change of Peking to Beijing and Mao Tse-tung to Mao Zedong. The *pinyin* version is much closer to the way Chinese people would say these words, and street signs in China are often written in *pinyin* as well as in characters.

Literature

Classic literature

China has one of the world's oldest literary traditions, dating back in a continuous line for more than three thousand years. One of the great early works was the *Shi Jing* (Book of Songs), dating from the eleventh to sixth century BCE. It is a collection of folk songs, some with a political theme, and ritual hymns, and was said to have been compiled by Confucius (c. 551–479 BCE, see pages 224–5). The *Shi Jing* is one of a group of revered texts associated with Confucius called the Confucian Classics, although he probably wrote none of them. Confucius's philosophy was preserved (or created) in the *Analects*, compiled by his disciples, such as Mencius, many centuries later. Dating from a similar time is Sun Zi's famous *The Art of War*, which advises on strategy and tactics in clear terms and is a great favourite with business people travelling to China today.

Very early on, poetry was seen as one of the highest forms of art, and the mark of an educated man. A government official was not expected to be merely good at his job, but a poet too. The distinctive allusive, enigmatic nature of Chinese poetry was already evident in the time of the Han dynasty (206 BCE–220 CE). But Chinese poetry reached its pinnacle in the time of the Tangs (618–907 CE) when the great poets Li Bai, Du Fu and Bai Juyi were writing. The hallmark of the Tang poems is the *shi* form, with its lines of five or seven characters, with the rhyme falling on even lines. The poems are typically wistful and melancholic, expressing sorrow at separation or exile. New forms of poetry were inspired by popular songs under, appropriately, the Song dynasty (960–1279). Under the Mings (1368–1644) many of the greatest poets were women.

Short stories began to flower in the Tang period, as well as poetry. Many survive, telling sad tales of lovers kept apart by fate or cruel parents, or of ardent young students striving to make their way up the career ladder but continually distracted by the highly seductive fox fairies (shape-shifting spirits who steal love from humans and then leave them to waste away). Gradually, the short story developed into the novel and by the middle of the Ming, there were great adventure yarns being written such as *Sanguo yanyi* (The Romance of the Three Kingdoms), a ripping historical novel about warriors and battles set in China's turbulent Three Kingdoms period 1,200 years earlier; *Shui hu zhuan* (All Men are Brothers, or The Water Margin), a stirring tale of Robin Hood-like bandits; and *Jin ping mei* (The Golden Lotus), a portrait of daily life in a wealthy family. The greatest of Chinese novels, though, was perhaps *Hong lou meng* (The Dream of the Red Chamber) from the Qing dynasty (1644–1911). Written by Cao Zhan and published posthumously in 1792, this huge, elaborate work is the original family saga, centring on the grandeur and decline of the Jia family. It is both a mystery story and a satire and follows the ups and downs in the lives of the volatile adolescent Jia Baoyu and his young female cousins Lin Daiyu and Xue Baochai.

Drama first developed under the Mongol emperors, the Yuan (1279–1368) and plays were written to be read as well as staged. The greatest Chinese playwright, though, was Tang Xianzu, who wrote epic romantic dramas.

Modern writing

In the twentieth century, many Chinese writers began to reject the elaborate, high-flown literary style of the classics and, in

1919, a group of them got together under the banner of the Fourth May Movement. Fourth May writers such as Lu Xun championed a more down-to-earth approach that reflected everyday spoken Chinese. In the 1930s, Shen Congwen began to write about ordinary people, with a sensitivity and insight that has been compared to that of Russian master Ivan Turgenev. The coming of Communism all but killed creative literature as the party refused to publish anything but socialist realism with its stirring tales of heroes battling for their country against the forces of imperialist corruption. Great novels were written during this time, such as the exposures of Zhang Ailing (Eileen Chang) of the cruelties of socialism, but they were not published in China until the 1990s. Lao She, one of China's greatest writers of the last century, was driven to suicide during the Cultural Revolution.

The freedom that came with the end of the Cultural Revolution in 1976, though, allowed a well of bitterness to bubble to the surface. Painful, highly personal stories that came to be called 'the literature of the wounded' began to express the terrible suffering of recent years. Often the official reaction to these works was shocked disbelief. Writer Bei Dao was told by police investigating the work of these scarred writers that it was impossible they had written such things themselves and that they must have been copied from foreigners. Nevertheless, this did not stop Wang Shuo's *Yearnings* being adapted into a 50-part TV soap opera in 1989.

Now, China's literature is as wide-ranging in style as western literature, though anything that is overtly critical of the leaders or the party is unlikely to find a publisher inside

China. Books such as Mo Yan's hard-hitting tale of rural life, *The Garlic Ballads,* for instance, are still banned in China. Salacious books, too, may find themselves under the baleful eye of the authorities, such as Wei Hui's *Shanghai Baby,* which the Chinese authorities tried to ban, and Chun Sue's *Beijing Doll,* the diaries of a teenage Beijing girl's sordid sexual encounters. In the West, many authors, especially women, have begun to make a mark with their explorations of the trials of life in twentieth-century China, such as Adeline Yen Mah's *Falling Leaves* and Jung Chang's *Wild Swans.* In China, though, the best-selling author today is Guo Jingming, who writes teenage tearjerkers.

Art

Classic painting

Painting and calligraphy were always the most highly esteemed arts in China. They were the amateur pursuits of those most revered of men, the gentlemen scholars, who cultivated this skill for intellectual and aesthetic satisfaction, not for a living.

Chinese paintings differ from their western counterparts in many ways, not least in their extreme simplicity. Many use little or no colour but are executed in ink of various shades. Even the most colourful use just subtle water colours, and are painted on nothing more durable than thin paper or silk, or on ceramics. Chinese paintings were not traditionally framed. Instead, they are painted on scrolls, on fans, in albums and on ceramics. So the composition is always in the form of exquisite, delicate cameos rather than frame-filling pictures.

The subject matter, too, is simple in range. Genuine abstracts are rare, and subjects rarely stray from the traditional array of landscapes, human figures, animals such as birds, and flowers. But within this narrow range, Chinese artists achieve an extraordinary variety, and each subject often has a symbolism that adds a meaning that is often lost on the western viewer. There are the flowers of the four seasons, for instance: the lotus for summer and purity; the peony for spring, wealth and honour; the chrysanthemum for autumn and venerable age; and *prunus* blossoms (plum, apricot, almond and cherry) for winter and beauty. Bamboo, *prunus* and pine, the 'three friends of winter' symbolise China's three main religions, Buddhism, Taoism and Confucianism.

Painting probably first began to flourish under the Han dynasty (206–220 BCE), and the Mawangdui banner, the first known silk painting, was found in a Han tomb. But little has survived from this time – partly because the huge imperial collection was destroyed during the civil war by soldiers who used the silk to make tents and bags, which must have been highly stylish! It was in the Tang dynasty, though, that painting really began to develop, and the great tradition of figure painting arose, as artists depicted great state occasions when the emperor received guests, or court ladies drifted elegantly hither and thither. The landscape, though, blossomed under the Song dynasty, and the landscape style of Song painters such as Su Dongpo has influenced Chinese artists ever since. The last Song emperor, Hui Zong, was himself a talented painter. There was a difference in approach, though, between the Northern Song period (960–1126) and the Southern Song (1126–1279). Northern Song paintings such as those of Xu Daoning showed nature dominant with monumental mountains dwarfing humans. Southern Song paintings, in contrast, allowed humans a much more prominent role, as in the twelfth-century *Walking on a Mountain Path in Spring*, in which all the non-essential landscape elements are left out.

It was under the Mongol Yuan emperors, however, that the idea of the amateur artist reached its apogee. Many Chinese officials were unwilling to serve under the alien Yuans, or were simply not wanted. So they retired to their homes and began to paint in a 'literati' style, exemplified by masters such as Zhao Mengfu, Huang Gongwang and Wu Zhen. These amateur painters cultivated the best of the Tang and Song with exquisite compositions of the simplest possible subjects such as *prunus* flowers. Ni Can, one of the great painters of the age, specialised in subtle ink paintings of bamboo plants. Interestingly, the simple symbolism of these paintings could hide a politically charged message. In 1306 Zheng Sixiao painted a simple painting of an orchid, which symbolised the high principles of a gentleman. But he painted it without roots – a subtle allusion to the theft of his land by the Mongol Yuans.

Under the Ming and Qing, the literati approach continued, and there are countless exquisite pictures of bamboo and *prunus* flowers, birds and landscapes, surviving from this period. But western influences began to creep in during the Qing dynasty, such as the Italian Castiglione (Lang Shi-ning) who concentrated on horses, dogs and flowers. The most famous artist of the period, though, is Qi Baishi (1863–1956), whose beautiful paintings of animals, insects and plants are so popular in the West.

The modern age

From the 1950s, of course, Chinese art, like literature, was dragooned into the cause of propaganda in the social realist style. For example, the artist Han Xin produced the most famous – and ubiquitous – picture of Chairman Mao. The persecution of artists reached its climax in the Cultural Revolution, and the end of the revolution saw a new generation of young artists bursting to express powerful feelings about the pain of persecution and dreams of a better future. A group of young artists who called themselves the Stars threw out all the traditions of Chinese art and began to experiment with a range of western styles from minimalism to cubism. Some of the Stars were young art students, but others were artists who had been driven to work in factories. Since no art gallery would show their work, they created their first exhibition by hanging their works on the railings of a small park near the National Art Museum in Beijing. The authorities were so shocked that the police came and tore them down, but the Stars had made their mark.

The 1980s saw a huge period of experimentation, especially with abstract art, in defiance of the Communist Party's attack on it for 'spiritual pollution'. Most of these radical efforts were western inspired, but in the 1990s, Chinese painters began to find their own approaches. Painters such as Liu Wei, Zhang Xiaogang and Fang Lijun began to paint in a bleak, often grotesque style that the famous art critic Li Xianting labelled 'cynical realism', while others began to play around with socialist-realist style. Wang Guangyi tellingly highlighted the dangers of the new capitalism by blending socialist-realist heroes with the logos of the multinationals moving in on China while other artists painted pop-art style images of Chairman Mao. This later style became something of a cliché as artists began to realize just how marketable this political art was in the West. Now Chinese art is moving more and more into the international mainstream, with lavish openings in stylish galleries in Beijing and Shanghai, and some Chinese artists commanding the kind of fees associated with the most sellable western artists.

Film

The history of cinema in China dates back to 1896, when a film was shown in a teahouse in Shanghai, and by the 1930s, Shanghai had a thriving cinema scene, fed partly by western imports for Shanghai's many foreigners, but also by a number of films made locally at studios such as the Mingxin and the Lianhua. The Shanghai films, though, never made much of an impact beyond the city's elite. Under Mao, of course, a whole raft of worthy films was churned out, but though they lacked quality, they introduced many Chinese people to cinema for the first time. Ticket sales rose from just 47 million in 1949 to a staggering 4 billion ten years later, as cinemas and film studios began springing up in every town. In the late 1950s, while Mao took a back seat, the government began to relax the rules on subjects suitable for film and some memorable films such as *Lin Zexu* were made. But by 1966, the Cultural Revolution had killed off this brief flowering of Chinese cinema.

With the end of the revolution, though, the Beijing Film Academy reopened and its graduates began what is called the Fifth Generation of film-making that has given Chinese cinema international acclaim. These Fifth Generation filmmakers abandoned socialist realism to explore the traditions and landscapes of pre-revolutionary China in grand style. The first was Chen Kaige and his cameraman Zhang Yimou's visually stunning film *Yellow Earth* (1982), with its vast and beautiful Shaanxi landscapes recalling Chinese paintings. This was followed by Zhang Yimou's epic *Red Sorghum* (1987) and Tian Zhuanzhuang's *Horse Thief. Red Sorghum*, which tells the story of heroic peasants defying Japanese armies in the 1940s, took Chinese audiences by storm and turned the film's lead actor Jiang Wen into a national star. Abroad, the film won huge acclaim and alerted western audiences to the arrival of Chinese cinema. It also made the film's leading actress, Gong Li, a heart-throb with many a young man in the West. Zhang Yimou and Gong Li became lovers and made many more hit films together, which cemented the growing reputation of Chinese cinema abroad, including *Judou*, *The Story of Qiu Ju* and *Raise the Red Lantern*. Zhang Yimou and Chen Kaige both seemed to reach their peaks in 1994, Zhang with *To Live* and Chen with *Farewell my Concubine*, both powerfully challenging and deeply emotional films set not in the distant past but in the twentieth century. Both film-makers, however, were then so comfortably embraced by the authorities, that many critics feel it has been their undoing. Chen Kaige went on to make the costliest Chinese film ever in *The Promise*, which many describe as an expensive flop, while Zhang Yimou has made a series of films most critics think are shallow crowd-pleasers, such as the martial-arts epic *The House of the Flying Daggers* (2004).

The problem for Chinese film-makers is that the official censors have a huge input into what is made and what is not, vetting not only funding but also all versions of the script and the film. The more challenging directors are faced with the dilemma of having their films cut to shreds by the censors or sending them uncut overseas and finding their work banned at home. One way round the censors now is to release the film on illegal DVDs. This is how Jia Zhangke's bleak *Xiao Wu* (Pickpocket, 1997) got its audience. Other banned films to spread like this are Jia's *The World* (2004) about workers fighting in Beijing and Yang Li's *Blind Shaft* (2003) about the dangers of rampant capitalism focusing on a murder cover-up at a coal mine. Interestingly, in 2006, Jia Zhangke was reha-bilitated and hired by the state to make edgy ads for the state mobile-phone company – featuring clips of his banned films!

Meanwhile, across the water in Hong Kong, there is a movie industry beaten for productivity only by Hollywood and India's Bollywood. It is in some ways out of reach of the official censors, but then has never really made films that are likely to cause many ripples anyway. The Hong Kong film-makers have got the high-speed, martial-arts action movie featuring stars such as Jackie Chan off to a tee – so much so that more artful western directors such as Ang Lee (*Crouching Tiger, Hidden Dragon*) and Quentin Tarantino have both made their *homage*. One Hong Kong director who has taken a different path is Wong Karwai, with intense, edgy films such as *Chungking Express* and *In the Mood for Love*.

SUGGESTED READING

Contemporary China

Getting Rich First Duncan Hewitt (Chatto & Windus, 2007)
   If you read one other book on China, make it this one

China: Friend or Foe? Hugo de Burgh (Icon Books, 2006)
China Inc Ted C Fishmann (Pocket Books/Simon & Schuster, 2006)
China's Democratic Future Bruce Gilley (Columbia University Press, 2004)
The Writing on the Wall Will Hutton (Little Brown, 2007)
China Shakes the World James Kynge (Weidenfeld & Nicolson, 2006)
New Cambridge Handbook of Contemporary China Colin Mackerras (Cambridge University Press, 2001)
China's New Rulers Andrew J Nathan and Bruce Gilley (New York Review, 2003)

The *Dragon and the Elephant* David Smith (Profile Books, 2007)
The China Dream Joe Studwell (Profile Books, 2002)
Behind the Wall Colin Thubron (Vintage, 2001)
The China Executive Wei Wang (2W Publishing, 2006)

Chinese history

The Changing Face of China John Gittings (Oxford, 2006)

Fiction and biography

The Rice Sprout Song Eileen Chang (University of California Press, 1998)
Wild Swans Jung Chang (HarperPerennial, 2004)
Shanghai Baby Wei Hui (Constable and Robinson, 2003)
Red Dust Ma Jian (Vintage, 2002)
Candy Mian Mian (Back Bay Books, 2003)
Playing for Thrills Wang Shuo (Penguin, 1998)
Yearnings Wang Shuo
Beijing Doll Chun Sue (Abacus, 2004)
Joy Luck Club Amy Tan (Vintage,1991)
Falling Leaves Adeline Yen Mah (Penguin, 1998)
The Story of Ah Q Lu Xun (Chinese University Press, 2002)

Classics

Romance of the Three Kingdoms Luo Guanzhong trans. CH Brewitt-Taylor (Tuttle Publishing, 2003)

Tao Te Ching Lao Tzu, trans. by Stephen Addiss and Stanley Lombardo (Hackett Publishing, 1993)

Art of War Sun Tzu, trans. Ralph Sawyer (Running Press Miniature Editions, 2003)

The Dream of the Red Chamber Cao Zhan trans. H Bencraft Joly (Dodo Press, 2007)

INDEX

2

195 - Children - not obeying teachers
         - respecting ...

111 - 1 in 60 own a car
      - coal primarily resp for pollution

      1 in 2 in Americas

Bill Hutton's "The writings of the
                     wall.
121
China in the World.

157 - taste of democracy